THE
KINGFISHER
HISTORY
ENCYCLOPEDIA

VOLUME 10
THE MODERN WORLD 1950–2000

KING*f*ISHER

KINGFISHER
Kingfisher Publications Plc
New Penderel House
283-288 High Holborn
London WC1V 7HZ

First published by Kingfisher Publications Plc in 1999
2 4 6 8 10 9 7 5 3 1
ITR/0599/CAC/UNV/128JDA

A CIP catalogue record for this book is available from
the British Library

ISBN 0 7534 0346 3

Printed in Hong Kong

PROJECT TEAM
Project Director and Art Editor Julian Holland
Editorial team Julian Holland, Norman Brooke
Designers Julian Holland, Nigel White/RWS Studio
Picture Research Anne-Marie Ehrlich, Josie Bradbury
Maps Jeffrey Farrow

FOR KINGFISHER
Managing Editor Miranda Smith
Art Director Mike Davis
DTP Co-ordinator Nicky Studdart
Artwork Research Katie Puckett
Production Manager Oonagh Phelan

CONTRIBUTORS
Teresa Chris, Neil Grant, Ken Hills, Julian Holland, Palden Jenkins,
Elizabeth Longley, Fiona Macdonald, Hazel Martell,
Mike McGuire, Theodore Rowland-Entwhistle

INTRODUCTION

Often, fact is stranger than fiction. Your *Kingfisher History Encyclopedia* is packed full of fascinating facts and real-life stories about the people, places and events of the past that have shaped the colourful but still turbulent world that we know today. The causes and effects of the actions and events are explained in full, giving a vivid picture of how leaders, tyrants, artists and scientists who lived hundreds of years ago have left a legacy which still impinges on people's lives at the beginning of the 21st century.

Use your *Kingfisher History Encyclopedia* to discover past events and find out how people have lived their lives over the last 40,000 years – from Stone Age cave-dwellers to the Anglo-Saxons, from the Aztecs and Incas of Central America to the Manchus in China, and from the American Revolutionary War to United Nations peace-keeping.

This user-friendly encyclopedia contains many features to help you look things up easily, or simply to have fun just browsing through. The in-depth coverage of each period of history also makes the encyclopedia perfect for all your project work and homework assignments.

The clear, informative text is accompanied by key date boxes, colourful photographs and superb illustrations and maps. At-a-glance world maps at the beginning of each chapter tell you quickly the major events that happened during a particular time period. These are arranged according to continent or area of the world. At the end of the chapters there are three special feature spreads which take an overall look at the arts, architecture, and science and technology of that particular period. And there is a Ready Reference section at the back of the book that contains lists of names and dates for quick and easy access.

Whether you use your *Kingfisher History Encyclopedia* for schoolwork or just to dip into at random, it will add considerably to your understanding of the past, and will stimulate you to explore further the lives of our ancestors.

THE MODERN WORLD

1950 – 2000

The years between 1950 and the present day are recent history. Some of the events may have occurred during our lifetime, or we may have seen reports of them on television. The latter half of the 20th century has seen social, technological and environmental changes on a scale never witnessed before. Politicians and policy-makers, as well as historians, have identified several important trends which will continue to transform our world: environmental pollution, ever-increasing populations, changing family structures, and a growing gap between rich and poor, people and countries.

▲ Aircraft carriers from Britain and the USA played an important peace-keeping role in the 1990s in various world trouble spots, such as the Middle East and Yugoslavia.

THE WORLD AT A GLANCE 1950–2000

This period was dominated by the Cold War between communist nations and the capitalist West. The United States and the USSR played leading parts. These two were also involved in the space race. The USSR was the first to send a man into space, and the USA the first to put a man on the Moon. Changes in the USSR led to the end of the Cold War but created uncertainty about the future as nationalists demanded independence.

In western Europe, the European Union encouraged economic growth and worked towards political union. In Africa, many nations became independent, but faced severe economic problems as well as droughts and famines. In southeast Asia, technology and industry developed, and Japanese business became the most successful in the world. China experienced a cultural revolution and Indochina was devastated by a whole series of wars.

NORTH AMERICA

This half-century was the high point of development of the USA, which led the way materially and culturally. By now, the US west coast was as much a centre for the film and aircraft industries as the east coast, and home to many futuristic ideas. The USA led the way in the nuclear arms race and was equal to the USSR in the space race. The 1950s saw growing prosperity, though this led to troubles in the 1960s over civil rights and social issues. American culture reached its high point in music, films, inventions and new ideas in the 1970s, though rocked by war in Vietnam and the exposure of government corruption. In the 1980s, computer technology and free-market economics brought economic boom, the space shuttle and the end of the Cold War. In the 1990s, Asia made great strides catching up, and USA became more multi-cultural. The USA acted as a global policeman in a complex world, and its internal politics have never been settled. Yet this was its greatest time in history. The American culture of Coca-Cola, Disney and Boeings spread to every corner of the world.

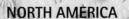

NORTH AMERICA

CENTRAL AND SOUTH AMERICA

CENTRAL AND SOUTH AMERICA

Until the 1970s, there was a battle between right-wing dictators and left-wing revolutionaries in Latin America. Poverty, power and guerrilla wars were the big issues. As the continent grew richer and more liberal governments came to power, these pressures eased. The Catholic Church also lost ground, and rainforest destruction, government corruption, human rights and the drugs trade grew as new issues. Civil wars in countries like Peru and Nicaragua were resolved, and in the 1990s Latin America, now industrialized, played an increasing role in global affairs.

EUROPE

Ruined by World War II and overshadowed by the Cold War, Europe made a dramatic recovery in the 1950s–1970s, beginning a long process of co-operation through the founding of the European Community. Europe worked with a 'social market' model of economics, with ample welfare and social systems which, by the 1990s, became a burden. Despite crises, such as the Hungarian uprising of 1956 and the 'Prague Spring' of 1968, Europe remained in peace. The greatest breakthrough was the ending of the Cold War, which reunited Germany and brought reconciliation between east and west, though ugly scenes such as the Yugoslavian civil wars of the 1990s hindered progress. Environmental and social concerns were important, especially after the Russian nuclear disaster at Chernobyl in 1986. Europe began to play a more equal role in the world community than in previous centuries.

ASIA

During this period, the fortunes of Asia rose again. The Maoist era in China brought mixed results, some impressive, some disastrous. They led to reforms in the 1980s and to China's re-entry into the world's market economy. Japan became the economic and technological powerhouse of Asia, and fuelled great economic growth in southeast Asia from the early 1970s. India modernized in the 1970s, though conflicts continued with Pakistan. The withdrawal of colonial powers, the Vietnam War, the rise of Islamic and Confucian values, the fall of the USSR in Central Asia and the globalization of the world economy have all had a great effect on Asia.

EUROPE

ASIA

MIDDLE EAST

AFRICA

AUSTRALASIA

Australia and New Zealand became leading countries, although they had to get used to being neighbours to Asia. Australia became one of the world's wealthiest countries. Polynesia became a tourist destination, but also a place for atomic bomb testing.

AUSTRALASIA

AFRICA

After a promising start in the 1960s, when most states gained independence, Africa was troubled with wars, corruption, famine and social crises. Foreign interference and over-exploitation were common. In South Africa, torn by apartheid, reform came in 1990 and brought the dawn of a new multi-racial society.t Africa remains troubled but lessons learned may lead to great future improvements.

MIDDLE EAST

Oil-rich, the Middle East witnessed great extremes of wealth and suffering during this period. Rising Islamic fundamentalism had mixed outcomes, disturbing peace, yet helping the poor and downtrodden. Caught between different world powers, war and interference by foreign powers were common.

THE COLD WAR 1945–1989

After the end of World War II, tensions between East and West and the build-up of nuclear weapons almost brought the world to the brink of a third world war.

Because of the serious threat of nuclear war between East and West during the 1960s, many Americans built fall-out shelters in their back gardens.

The USSR and the USA fought together as allies against Germany and Japan in World War II, but in 1945, these two great countries, known as superpowers, became rivals and then enemies. This division became known as the Cold War, a war conducted in the main without fighting. The USA and USSR 'fought' by making threats and by strengthening their armed forces.

Both countries built up an enormous stockpile of nuclear weapons. Peaceful, friendly contacts between their peoples ceased. The USSR became completely shut off from the rest of the world by Soviet troops. The British statesman Sir Winston Churchill memorably described the frontier between East and West as an 'iron curtain' in a speech that he gave in Missouri, USA, on March 5, 1946.

The Cold War dominated world politics for many years. On one side, the United States became the leader of NATO, a military alliance of Western nations ranged against the communist powers. On the other side, the USSR dominated the Warsaw Pact, a military alliance of East European states that backed communism.

A 1962 cartoon, produced at the time of the Cuba missile crisis, shows the two superpower leaders arm-wrestling for power. The USSR's Nikita Khrushchev (1894–1971), on the left, faces the US president John F. Kennedy (1917–63). They are both sitting on their own nuclear weapons.

BERLIN: THE DIVIDED CITY

In 1945, the USA, France and Britain took control of West Germany and the USSR controlled East Germany. The capital, Berlin, inside East Germany,was also divided, and in 1948, the Soviets closed all access to west Berlin. The Western powers brought in essential supplies by air until the Russians lifted the blockade in May 1949. From 1949 to 1958, three million people escaped from east to west Berlin. In 1961, East Germany closed off this escape route by building the Berlin Wall through the centre of the city. It crossed tramlines and roads, and created an area on either side known as no man's land.

▲ The Berlin Wall, built in 1961 to divide east and west Berlin, finally fell in November 1989.

▶ By 1949, most European states had joined rival alliances. Warsaw pact countries supported the USSR. Members of NATO backed the USA.

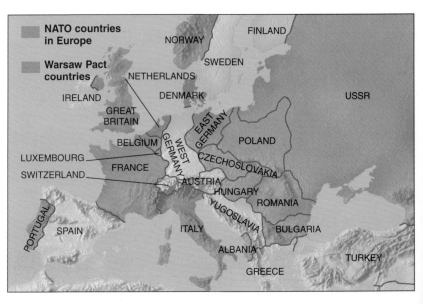

NATO countries in Europe

Warsaw Pact countries

FINLAND
NORWAY
SWEDEN
NETHERLANDS
IRELAND
DENMARK
USSR
GREAT BRITAIN
EAST GERMANY
BELGIUM
WEST GERMANY
POLAND
LUXEMBOURG
CZECHOSLOVAKIA
FRANCE
SWITZERLAND
AUSTRIA
HUNGARY
ROMANIA
PORTUGAL
YUGOSLAVIA
SPAIN
ITALY
BULGARIA
ALBANIA
TURKEY
GREECE

CUBAN MISSILE CRISIS

Although the USA and the USSR never
actually fought, they came close to it.
The world held its breath for a whole
week in October 1962 when the US
president, John F. Kennedy, received air
force photographs showing that the USSR
was building missile launch sites in Cuba.
From there, the nuclear missiles could
reach and destroy many US cities. On
October 22, the president ordered a naval
blockade of Cuba. The United States
made plans to invade Cuba, and the
world braced itself for nuclear war. Finally,
on October 28, Nikita Khrushchev, the
Soviet leader, backed down and agreed to
remove the missiles and destroy the
Cuban launch sites. The crisis was over.

THE END OF THE COLD WAR

In the 1980s, the friendly relationship
between US president Ronald Reagan
and the Soviet leader Mikhail Gorbachev
helped to reduce Cold War tensions, and
by 1987, they had agreed to abolish
medium-range nuclear missiles. In 1989,
Gorbachev allowed the communist
countries of eastern Europe to elect
democratic governments, and in 1991,
the USSR broke up into 15 republics. The
Cold War was over. On March 12, 1999,
Hungary, Poland and the Czech Republic
joined NATO. The joining ceremony was
held at the Harry S. Truman
memorial library in
Independence, Missouri,
in the United States.

◀ Francis Gary Powers
was the pilot of an
American U-2 spy plane
which was shot down
over Soviet territory in
1960. He was released
in exchange for the
imprisoned Soviet
spymaster Rudolf Abel.

▼ Czech students tried
to stop Soviet tanks in
Prague, in August 1968.
The USSR feared that
independent actions by
Warsaw Pact members
might weaken its power,
so the Russians moved
into Czechoslovakia.

▶ During the Cold War,
many groups of people,
such as the Peace Pledge
Union, were formed to try
and influence governments
and stop the spread of
nuclear weapons.

PEACE?

PEACE PLEDGE UNION

◀ Supporters of the
Campaign for Nuclear
Disarmament (CND)
marched through London
in 1983 to demonstrate
against the deployment of
Cruise and Trident nuclear
missiles on British soil.

IN SPACE 1957–2000

Space exploration began in 1957 when the USSR launched Sputnik I, the first artificial satellite to orbit the Earth. In 1969, the first man walked on the Moon.

The development of technology during World War II helped scientists to realize that one day it might be possible for people to travel in space. Cold War rivalry between the USA and the USSR triggered a space race. Both sides felt that being the first nation in space would increase their prestige. They also hoped that space science would help them develop new, more powerful weapons.

The Soviets achieved the first 'space first' when they sent a satellite into orbit around the Earth in 1957. Soon, both sides were investing enormous amounts of time and money in space science. The Soviets achieved another space first in 1961 when Yuri Gagarin became the first man in space. Other notable achievements by both countries included probes being sent to the Moon and past Venus, further manned flights, spacewalks and the launch of communications satellites.

The Apollo programme of space flights enabled the USA to land men on the Moon. Between July 1969 and December 1972, the USA successfully carried out six of these missions, the last three involving the use of a Lunar Roving Vehicle.

Sputnik 1 was launched by Russia on October 4, 1957. The satellite was used to broadcast scientific data and orbited the Earth for six months.

Russian cosmonaut Yuri Gagarin in the cabin of *Vostok 1*, the spacecraft in which he became the first person to orbit the Earth on April 12, 1961.

In the run-up to the Apollo flights, the American Gemini programme was designed to teach astronauts how to cope with space travel. In November 1966 'Buzz' Aldrin carried out three spacewalks high over the Earth.

The ending of the Cold War and the economic crisis of the 1970s led the two superpowers to scale down their space programme. However, the Soviets gained valuable experience with long-endurance flights on permanent space stations. Co-operation between the two countries is important for the future construction of an international space station.

MAN ON THE MOON

In 1961, the United States president, John F. Kennedy, said that his scientists would send a man to the Moon by 1970. In fact, the first manned Moon landing took place on July 20, 1969 with the American *Apollo 11* mission. The crew consisted of Neil Armstrong, the first man to set foot on the Moon, Edwin 'Buzz' Aldrin, who was the second man to walk on the Moon, and Michael Collins who remained in lunar orbit in the command and service module. Armstrong described walking on the Moon as "one small step for a man, one giant leap for mankind".

◄ *Apollo 11* was launched from Cape Canaveral, Florida, on July 16, 1969 and made the first manned landing on the Moon just four days later.

SPACE SHUTTLES

In the USA, the National Aeronautics & Space Administration (NASA) required a reusable space vehicle to construct and serve planned space stations. The space shuttle could take off like a rocket – with a large payload – and return to Earth like a plane. The launch of the first shuttle in 1981 marked a new phase in space exploration. Since that first flight, space shuttles have carried a variety of payloads and retrieved and repaired satellites. In 1995, the space shuttle *Atlantis* docked with the Russian space station *Mir*, marking an important step forward in international co-operation.

▲ This picture of the dusty, rock-strewn surface of Mars, was taken by one of the two US Viking landers in 1975. Part of the spacecraft is visible in the foreground.

The Soviet space station *Mir* was launched in 1986. It was designed to stay in orbit for long periods, so that complicated scientific experiments could be carried out on board. It has now far exceeded its planned life. Although it requires fairly constant repair and maintenance, the station is still manned after 13 years' service.

EXPLORING DEEP SPACE

Unmanned space probes have flown by, or landed on, every planet in the solar system except Pluto. Soviet probes succeeded in landing on Venus in 1975 and sent back pictures. In 1976, two US Viking craft landed on Mars and began observations that lasted for six years. In 1977, the US launched the two Voyager missions which travelled round the solar system using the 'slingshot' technique – the spacecraft being flung from planet to planet by their gravitational fields. Before they disappeared into deep space, they transmitted valuable data and colour photographs of Jupiter, Saturn, Uranus and Neptune.

The Hubble space telescope, launched by the US in 1990, enabled scientists to produce high-resolution images of objects billions of light years way, and provided valuable information about the Universe.

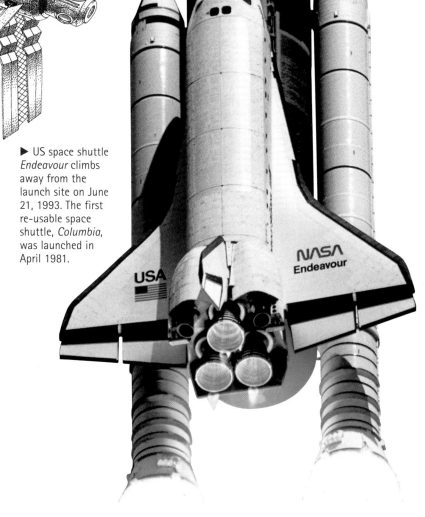

▶ US space shuttle *Endeavour* climbs away from the launch site on June 21, 1993. The first re-usable space shuttle, *Columbia*, was launched in April 1981.

439

CHINA 1949–1997

In 1949, Mao Zedong and the communist party came to power and transformed this battle-weary country. Full political freedom has still not yet been achieved.

By the 1990s, China was far removed from its previous peasant economy. All types of sophisticated electronic equipment were now being manufactured and exported abroad.

▼ Mao Zedong tried to solve the problem of food shortages in China by creating collective farms. Nevertheless, the country continued to suffer periods of extreme food shortage.

The communist party came to power in China in 1949, and Mao Zedong, their leader, became chairman of the Peoples' Republic of China. Civil war, and the war with Japan, had left the land poor and many people were starving. Roads, railways, schools and hospitals could not meet the peoples' needs. Many in the new government believed that they should follow the example of the communists in Russia. Mao did not agree with the move to industrialization, because he believed in a peasant economy. Land was redistributed to the peasants but a huge bureaucracy was also created. Mao resigned in 1959.

While the government followed the Russian example, Mao started his own 'Cultural Revolution' in 1965, aimed at attacking the party leaders. In 1970, he was made supreme commander.

Mao transformed Chinese society. Collective farms grew basic foods and industry produced more iron and steel.

To reduce the population, the Chinese government encouraged couples to have only one child. More recently, it made having more than one child illegal.

'Barefoot doctors' provided medical care to people in the countryside and children learned to read and write. Mao wrote and distributed widely 'The Thoughts of Chairman Mao'. It was required reading and everyone carried a copy with them wherever they went. Even the simplest peasants were able to quote from it.

TIANANMEN SQUARE

Despite the Chinese government's demands that the students stop their protest, on May 4, 1989, around 100,000 students and workers marched to Tiananmen Square in Beijing and demanded political reform. The government declared martial law on May 20, and finally, on June 3–4, the People's Liberation Army and its tanks moved in to end the protest. It is believed that more than three thousand protesters were killed and another ten thousand injured, although actual figures may never be known. Many people did died and many more were imprisoned. Western nations were shocked by the brutality with which the Chinese government dealt with the students, and strong diplomatic protests were made.

▲ This picture of a lone student standing in the path of the tanks was seen on television all around the world.

CIVIL RIGHTS

Many of Mao's political opponents were executed, scholars were imprisoned and tortured, families were split up, and yet millions of people still died from famine. During the Cultural Revolution, Mao was reacting because many educated people had criticized communism in the early 1960s. He was afraid that they would resist the imposition of his extreme form of communism.

After Mao's death in 1976, the Chinese government gradually became more open and began to encourage contacts with the rest of the world. Industry in China became more important and the government allowed some foreign investment because they saw the benefits of exporting to the rest of the world. It was because of this world trade that it was important for China to be seen to be giving its people more civil rights. However, the massacres that followed student demonstrations in Tiananmen Square, in Beijing in 1989, showed full political freedom had not been achieved.

POPULATION GROWTH

China saw a massive increase in its population which had reached over 1,200,000,000 by 1990. In an effort to achieve a stable population by around the year 2000 the government rewarded one-child families with priority housing and medical care. This scheme has been relatively successful.

▼ A magnificient fireworks display marked the return of Hong Kong to Chinese ownership on June 30, 1997 when Britain's 99-year lease on the territory officially came to an end.

WORLD ECONOMY 1950–2000

The industrialized countries of the world had improved their standard of living since 1950, but many poorer countries saw little or no improvement.

The OECD (Organization for Economic Co-operation and Development) was created to protect weak nations from powerful market forces and aid economic development.

The flag of the European Union, the successor to the European Economic Community first formed after the two Treaties of Rome in March 1957. The EU currently includes 15 member states.

▼ There was panic trading on the floor of the New York Stock Exchange in October 1987. In that year, stockmarkets around the world suffered a dramatic downward revaluation in the value of shares.

After the end of World War II, the USA and many countries in western Europe enjoyed a rapid growth in their economies. After the war, there was an enormous amount of re-building to be done, particularly in Europe. There was full employment and the amount people were paid, compared to what things cost to buy, steadily climbed. This rise in 'standard of living' also applied to a slightly lesser extent to countries such as Australia and New Zealand, as well as southeast Asian states such as Hong Kong, Singapore and Taiwan.

This prosperity came to a sudden halt in 1973 when the price of crude oil started to increase. The Organization of Petroleum Exporting Countries (OPEC) was founded in 1960 to get the best price on world markets for its member states' oil. OPEC members include many Middle Eastern Arab states as well as Venezuela, Algeria, Indonesia, Nigeria and the Gabon. Between 1973 and 1974, OPEC quadrupled the price of oil, and this led to a worldwide energy crisis. Poorer nations were badly hit by the rise in oil prices. By 1981, this had increased almost twenty times and their economies had to be supported by loans from the West. In the advanced nations, the energy crisis caused inflation, because the rise in oil prices was passed on in the form of raised prices for goods, and unemployment everywhere rose as less goods were exported.

COMMON MARKETS

Throughout the world, neighbouring states, or states with shared economic interests, have joined together to form powerful international associations. Some groups of states have also set up economic communities known as 'common markets'. Within these markets, members buy and sell at favourable rates. They agree to protect one another from economic competition from the outside.

In Asia, there are the Asia-Pacific Economic Co-operation Group (APEC) and the Association of Southeast Asian Nations (ASEAN). The North American Free Trade Agreement (NAFTA), originally the US and Canada, now includes Mexico. The Group of Seven, or G-7, is a group of major countries that meets to monitor the world economic situation. The European Community (EU) is the successor of the European Economic Community (EEC) of the 1950s. It has 15 members and forms a significant world trading-block. There are currently plans for a single European currency, as well as taxation and legal systems.

The collapse of the Soviet Union in the early 1990s meant that the former communist countries had to compete with other third world countries. While the richer Western nations provided aid to poorer countries in the past, they remained reluctant to share a substantial part of their wealth or expertise.

By the 1990s, it was estimated that the world's oil reserves amounted to around 700 billion barrels, of which 360 billion barrels were to be found in the Middle East.

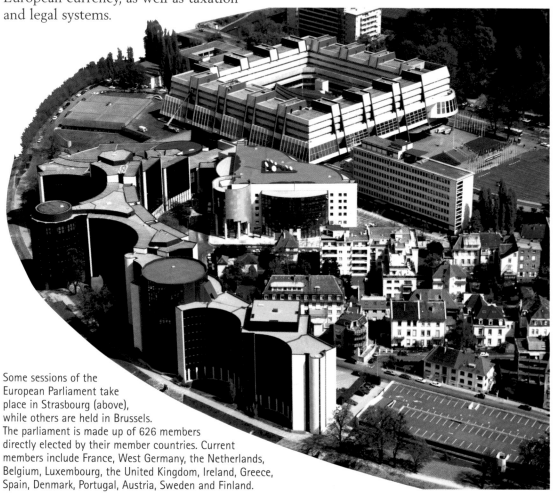

Some sessions of the European Parliament take place in Strasbourg (above), while others are held in Brussels. The parliament is made up of 626 members directly elected by their member countries. Current members include France, West Germany, the Netherlands, Belgium, Luxembourg, the United Kingdom, Ireland, Greece, Spain, Denmark, Portugal, Austria, Sweden and Finland.

▲ The European Currency Unit (ECU) is the proposed currency that will be used by members of the European Union instead of their own individual currencies.

WARS IN ASIA 1950–1988

Japan's defeat and the collapse of colonial rule led to fighting between political rivals throughout Asia. The superpowers took sides and began to join in.

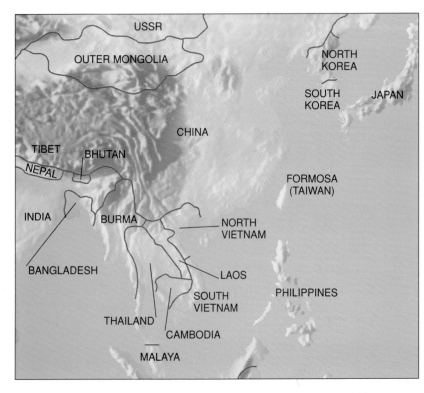

Australian soldiers were part of the United Nations forces that by the end of 1950 had pushed the North Koreans back as far as the border with China.

▼ Fighting between rival political groups flared up in many parts of Asia between 1946 and 1988 following Japan's defeat in World War II and the collapse of European colonial power.

In 1950, many countries in the East had still not recovered from Japanese invasions during World War II. People needed peace and stability, but many nations were at war. These wars caused further damage to people, cities and the land. Eastern countries no longer wished to be colonies of distant European powers. And the old colonial masters (France, Britain and the Netherlands) wanted to hold on to these potentially rich lands.

Fighting broke out in Vietnam and its neighbours Laos, Thailand and Cambodia, as well as in Indonesia, Malaysia, Burma and the Philippines. These wars were often complicated by political differences between rival groups seeking independence. The situation became more dangerous still when the Soviet, Chinese and American superpowers joined in with offers of money, weapons or technical advice for one side or the other.

In 1945, French colonial rule was restored to Vietnam. French Foreign Legion troops were sent to North Vietnam in 1953 to try to suppress a communist uprising.

THE KOREAN WAR

The Korean War began when communist North Korea attacked South Korea in June 1950. The United Nations quickly authorized its members to aid South Korea. The United States, together with 16 other countries, began sending in troops. Within two months, North Korean troops had captured most of South Korea. In September 1950, UN forces mounted a massive land, sea and air assault at Inchon, near Seoul. The UN troops recaptured most of South Korea and advanced into the North. By November, they had reached the North Korean border with China. Chinese troops then entered the fighting and forced the UN forces to retreat south. A ceasefire ended the war in July 1953.

▲ Between 1948 and 1960, British troops were sent to Malaya to fight the communist guerrilla offensive. Here, soldiers of a jungle patrol rest under a temporary shelter.

During the Vietnam War (1964–75), many parts of the country were devastated. Thousands of civilians were killed, and others were made homeless and fled as refugees to neighbouring countries. Peace finally came in 1976 when Vietnam was united.

Ho-Chi Minh (1892–1969) was a founder member of the French Communist Party and a revolutionary Vietnamese leader. He led the struggle against the French colonial rule of Vietnam and American-supported South Vietnam.

WAR IN VIETNAM

After the French were defeated by Vietnamese communists in 1954, the country was temporarily divided into two – north and south. Planned elections for the country did not take place and the communists in the north started giving aid to South Vietnamese communists, the Viet Cong, to help them overthrow the government of Ngo Dinh Diem.

In 1965, the United States sent the first troops to help the south and by 1969 there were more than half a million US troops in Vietnam. After Richard Nixon became US president in 1969, he began to withdraw troops. A ceasefire was signed in 1973, and the remainder of American soldiers went home. During the war, more than 57,000 Americans were killed or went missing in action.

CIVIL WAR IN CAMBODIA

In Cambodia, a guerrilla army, the Khmer Rouge, was led by Pol Pot, and they sought to overthrow the government of Lon Nol. The Khmer Rouge took over Cambodia in 1975 and Pol Pot became prime minister. His terror regime ended in 1978 when he was overthrown by Vietnamese troops.

▲ After Richard Nixon (1913–94) became president in 1969, he began to withdraw US troops from Vietnam. In 1973, a ceasefire was signed and the US troops were withdrawn.

◄ In Cambodia, Pol Pot (1926–98) was the leader of the Khmer Rouge guerrillas. They fought a long civil war beginning in 1963, and finally took over the country in 1975. Over the following three years, it is estimated that between two and four million people were executed or died of famine and disease.

KEY DATES	
1950	North Korean forces invade South Korea
1953	Ceasefire in Korea
1954	Vietminh communists defeat the French and Vietnam is divided
1963	Civil war starts in Cambodia
1965	First US troops land in Vietnam
1969	Richard Nixon becomes US president
1973	All US troops withdrawn from Vietnam
1975	Pol Pot takes over Cambodia
1979	Pol Pot deposed by Vietnamese forces
1993	First free elections in Cambodia for 20 years

CIVIL RIGHTS 1950–2000

Civil rights are the basic freedoms and rights of people living within a community. The rights are guaranteed by laws and customs that give everyone fair treatment.

Re-formed during the 1950s, the Ku Klux Klan harassed blacks and minority groups in the USA. They burned crosses to intimidate people.

The idea of civil rights in the West dates back to the writings of many Ancient Greek and Roman philosophers and to the ideas of Judaism and Christianity. In some countries, civil rights are protected by a written constitution. In the USA and in other democratic countries, such as the United Kingdom, they consist of laws and customs built up over hundreds of years.

Civil rights mean that people must be treated fairly and equally, no matter what their sex, religion or ethnic origin. They should be given the freedom to express what they believe in speech or in the media. They should also have the right to organize a political party, to have a fair trial and to vote in elections. Many oppressive regimes still ignore civil rights and abuse their power.

During 1989, Chinese students demonstrated in Beijing, demanding democracy in their country. The government sent in the army and thousands of students were killed.

Many rights have been won only after a long and painful struggle. During the 1950s and 1960s, Dr Martin Luther King led the civil rights campaign in the USA to win equality for black Americans.

In the early 1960s, many southern US states operated a colour bar. This taxi was only for the use of coloured people. Other forms of public transport were similarly segregated.

MARTIN LUTHER KING

The Reverend Martin Luther King Jr (1929–68) was a Baptist minister and the leader of the US civil rights movement of the 1950s and 1960s. On August 28, 1963, he led a march on Washington DC where he gave a famous speech that began, 'I have a dream...' His dream was of a future in which his country would live by the ideals of freedom and liberty on which it had been founded. On April 4, 1968, he was shot dead by James Earl Ray. From 1983, the third Monday in January has been designated a federal holiday in his honour.

CIVIL RIGHTS ABUSES

In South Africa, Nelson Mandela was sent to prison in 1962 for opposing apartheid (the separation of whites and non-whites). Many governments and people from all over the world campaigned to end apartheid by holding demonstrations, boycotting goods from South Africa and stopping all sporting links. F. W. de Klerk became president in 1989 and he began to dismantle apartheid. Mandela was released in 1990, the year apartheid was abolished. In 1994, he was elected South Africa's first black president.

In 1976, Argentina was taken over by a military junta. They suppressed opposition by arresting thousands of people and holding them in prison without trial. Between 20,000 and 30,000 people were never seen again and they became known by their families as '*los desaparecidos*', the 'disappeared ones'. Similar brutality was used by the military regime led by General Pinochet in Chile between 1973 and 1990.

PROTECTING CIVIL RIGHTS

International bodies, such as the United Nations and the European Court of Human Rights, protect civil rights. Other organizations, such as Amnesty International, campaign on behalf of people who are persecuted. However, some governments continue to obstruct civil rights. Dictators and single-party states deny rights to ordinary people because they see them as a threat.

▲ In the 1970s and 1980s, Chile was ruled by a military junta. Ordinary citizens were arrested and many were never seen again. The Catholic Church denounced the violence against innocent people. They held religious services for detained or missing people.

◀ In the South African city of Johannesburg in the 1980s, many black and coloured people were moved into slums and shanty towns to make more room for the homes of white people.

When European settlers first arrived in Australia in the 18th and 19th centuries, the Aborigines, the original inhabitants of the land, were driven off their traditional hunting grounds. Many also died from European diseases brought in by the settlers. At the end of the 20th century, the Australian government still does not recognize that the Aborigines were the original custodians of the land before European settlers arrived in 1788.

TERRORISM 1952–2000

During the latter half of the 20th century, many people used violence to promote particular political causes, often aimed at overthrowing the established order.

During 1981, some members of the Irish Republican Army (IRA) who were serving prison sentences in Northern Ireland for terrorist offences went on hunger strike. When one of them died, there was rioting.

▼ In 1988, an American jumbo jet was blown up by a bomb in mid-air over the Scottish town of Lockerbie, killing 270 people. Terrorists were suspected of being responsible for this act.

Some groups of people use violence (terrorism) to gain publicity and win support for a political cause. They are often called freedom fighters by their supporters. Terrorists murder and kidnap people, set off bombs and hijack aircraft. The reasons behind terrorism are not always the same. Some people want to spread their own political beliefs while others (nationalists or liberationists) want to establish a separate state for peoples who do not have a country of their own. For example, in the Middle East, terrorists have kidnapped people and carried out bombing campaigns to draw attention to the cause of the Palestinian people who do not have a homeland.

In Spain, an extreme group, *Euzkada Ta Askatasuna* (ETA) began a terrorist campaign in the 1960s to pressurize the government into creating a separate state for the Basque people. Similarly, in Northern Ireland, Nationalist groups such as the Irish Republican Army (IRA) escalated their terrorist campaign in the 1970s against British rule in the province.

In April 1995, a bomb exploded and destroyed the Federal Office building in Oklahoma City, USA. This was one of very few terrorist attacks on the North American mainland.

During the 1970s, the Red Army Faction were involved in acts of violence in West Germany. They robbed banks, and in 1977, kidnapped and murdered a businessman, Hans-Martin Schleyer. They were also involved in acts of terrorism carried out by Palestinians, including the murder of Israeli athletes at the 1972 Olympic Games in Munich. In Italy, in 1978, terrorists called the Red Brigade kidnapped and murdered the former prime minister of Italy, Aldo Moro.

Most governments around the world reject terrorist demands because they fear that to give in would only encourage other terrorists to commit violence.

FAMINE IN AFRICA 1967–2000

Africa has suffered periodic drought and famine since ancient times. More recently, civil war in newly independent states has only added to the misery.

In 1985, the pop musician Bob Geldof organized the Live Aid music concerts. These raised £50 million to help the victims of the famine in Ethiopia.

Widespread famines have occurred periodically in most parts of sub-Saharan Africa since ancient times. Factors such as a failure of the annual rains, poor soil conditions and negligible food reserves have all played a part in these tragedies. Following independence, in the latter half of the 20th century, civil wars have added to the misery.

CIVIL UNREST AND FAMINE

Most of the worst famines during this period happened in countries that suffered civil unrest. In Nigeria, the people who lived in the east of the country were the Christian Ibo tribe. They were oppressed by the majority Islamic Hausa and Fulani peoples. When tens of thousands of Ibos were massacred, the Eastern Region declared its independence as the state of Biafra in May 1967. War continued between the two sides until January 1970. It is believed that more than a million Biafrans died because the Nigerians stopped emergency food getting through.

▼ Zaire has had periods of military uprising and civil strife which has made life dangerous for foreign aid workers. In 1994, the arrival of hundreds of thousands of refugees from neighbouring Rwanda prompted massive aid from international relief agencies.

Civil strife in Mozambique in the 1980s led to the almost total collapse of health care, education and food production. By the beginning of the 1990s, nearly a million people had died and another million and a half had fled and were refugees in neighbouring countries.

During the 1991–93 civil war in Somalia, it is thought that about 300,000 people starved to death because the war made it too dangerous to deliver food aid.

Ethiopia suffered from drought and famine for many years. Between 1977 and 1991, the combination of civil war and famine killed millions of Ethiopians.

In Ethiopia, the combination of the withdrawal of aid from the USSR, drought and a civil war in the 1970s and 1980s led to millions of people dying from famine. Through the Western media, people all round the world became aware of the catastrophe. International relief charities, such as the Red Cross and Oxfam, the Live Aid pop concerts of 1985 and various governments all provided vast amounts of aid for the victims.

▲ Foreign aid is not only used to provide food for the starving people of Africa. This project provided clean water for a community in Kenya. Projects like this help to improve the health of the local people.

NEW NATIONS 1950–1996

Following centuries of rule by colonial powers, many nations have gained their independence – achieved through war, terrorism or more peaceful means.

Independence was granted to Ghana (formerly the Gold Coast) by Britain in 1957. The Duchess of Kent represented the British queen at the ceremony in the capital, Accra. In the following years, the country suffered from government corruption and military coups.

After World War II, the leaders of many European-ruled colonial countries felt the growing pressure from their people for independence from their foreign 'masters'. The days of colonial rule were rapidly coming to an end. During the 1950s and 1960s, many peoples in Africa and southeast Asia fought for their independence. Their people believed that they had a right to own and control their own countries. Many of these independence movements were led by men and women of courage and vision. They were frequently imprisoned, but in some cases eventually gained power.

Many of these countries used military force to win independence from colonial rule. European nations would not give up their power and so groups like the Mau Mau in Kenya launched terrorist campaigns. In some states, for example Egypt in 1952–53, independence was achieved only after the army took control.

The British gained control of Malaya in 1786. In September 1963, Malaya, Singapore, Sarawak and Sabah joined together to create the independent Federation of Malaysia. Singapore left the organization two years later.

RANDOM BORDERS

In Africa, numerous civil wars sprung up as the European powers gradually withdrew. One of the most common reason for this was that, where the land had been previously divided up between the European settlers, little attention was paid to the existing tribal boundaries. When the Europeans left, several tribes were often left to dispute the ownership and control of that country. When this happened in Nigeria, with the declaration of an independent Biafran state in 1967, millions of people died of starvation.

Britain granted full independence to Nigeria in 1960. Since then the country, one of the largest in Africa and a major oil producer, has suffered from a major civil war, economic problems and the restrictions of military rule.

STRUGGLE FOR SURVIVAL

Today, nearly all the former colonies are independent. Some maintain ties, as do members of the British Commonwealth. Others, such as the Organization for African Unity (OAU), have formed new alliances. Many former colonies are still economically dependent. World trade is controlled by Europe, the USA and Japan, as well as by multinational companies. It is hard for new nations not to fall into debt when they do not have financial control.

Turkmenistan, on the eastern coast of the Caspian Sea, became a republic of the USSR in 1925. Following the break-up of the Soviet Union in 1991, this mainly Muslim country declared independence and joined the Commonwealth of Independent States (CIS), consisting of 12 of the 15 former Soviet republics.

EASTERN EUROPE

The end of the Cold War and the collapse of the USSR at the end of the 1980s led to the countries around Russia's borders gaining their freedom from Soviet rule. In Czechoslovakia, free elections were held in 1990 for the first time since 1946. At the beginning of 1993, Czechoslovakia ceased to exist and was replaced by the states of the Czech Republic and Slovakia.

Following the death of President Tito in 1980, Yugoslavia soon became divided. Macedonia, Croatia, Slovenia and Bosnia–Herzegovina all declared independence. Their different ethnic groups fought each other, and in the wars that followed, thousands of people were either killed or made homeless and became refugees.

▲ After the break-up of the USSR in 1991, the Muslim state of Uzbekistan became independent and joined the Commonwealth of Independent States (CIS). Food shortages in 1992 led to civil unrest and riots in the capital, Tashkent.

◄ Bosnia and Herzegovina became part of what was to be known as Yugoslavia at the end of World War I. Nationalist feeling grew after the death of President Tito in 1980. Independence was declared in 1992 against the wishes of the Serbian population and a bitter civil war broke out. Many people lost their homes and became refugees.

WARS IN THE MIDDLE EAST 1956–2000

Following the formation of the state of Israel in 1948 there have been many tensions in the Middle East that have led to bitter disputes and even war.

The Six Day War took place June 5–10, 1967. In a surprise attack, Israeli bombers destroyed Egyptian planes, and then sent in troops to capture the Egyptian soldiers left in Sinai.

▼ The Yom Kippur War began in 1973 when Egypt and Syria launched a surprise attack on Israel after it refused to give up land captured during the Six Day War.

There have been many conflicts in the Middle East between Israeli, Palestinian and Arab peoples, particularly since 1948. Some areas of territory are still in dispute.

The lands around Jerusalem have been believed for centuries by Jews to be the traditional home of the Jewish people. After World War II, many Jewish refugees settled in Palestine although the area was occupied by Arab peoples. The state of Israel was formed in 1948 and fighting broke out with neighbouring Arab countries and continued on and off for many years. In 1956, Egypt took over the control of the Suez Canal which was owned by Britain and France. Because it felt threatened, Israel invaded Egyptian territory in Sinai, and Britain and France attacked the canal area. There was international disapproval, and the USA and the USSR both called for a ceasefire. UN troops moved in to keep the peace after the withdrawal of Israeli, British and French troops.

Tensions continued to grow in the 1960s between Israel and the Arab countries of Egypt, Jordan and Syria. They were aided by several other Arab countries including Iraq, Kuwait, Saudi Arabia, Algeria and Sudan. Both sides were hostile and unwilling to negotiate differences. Both sides were also occupied with preparing their troops for a possible armed conflict. In May 1967, Egypt closed the Gulf of Aqaba to Israeli shipping.

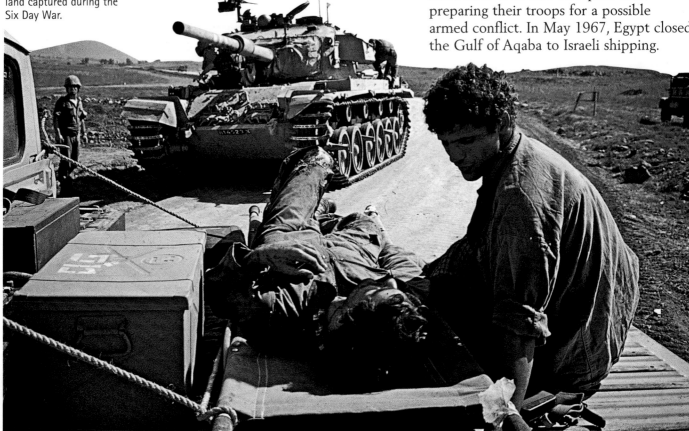

In 1980, Iraq invaded Iraq. The two countries fought a long and bitter war which was not to end until August 1988 and which cost the lives of over a million of their soldiers, with nearly two million wounded.

THE SIX DAY WAR

In June 1967, the Israeli air-force launched a surprise air attack on the Arab forces' air bases which put them completely out of action. Over a period of six days, the Israelis moved their army to occupy the Gaza Strip and parts of the Sinai. They also pushed back the border with Jordan and captured the Golan Heights from Syria.

IRAQI AGRESSION

In 1979, the Shah of Iran was deposed and replaced by Islamic fundamentalist Shiite Muslims led by the Ayatollah Khomeini. Tensions between Iran and Iraq finally resulted in Iraq invading the oil-rich Iranian territory of Khuzistan in 1980. Iraq feared the power of the new Iranian government set up by Ayatollah Khomeini. When the war ended in 1988, neither country had made any gains, but the cost to two nations was over a million dead with nearly two million injured.

Rivalries within the Arab world have often been caused by the region's oil deposits. In 1990, Iraq invaded Kuwait in order to improve its sea access. The UN Security Council passed several resolutions that demanded that Iraq immediately withdraw its troops. When Saddam Hussein refused, a multinational force led by the Americans forced him to withdraw. Kuwait City was liberated within the first five days and thousands of Iraqi soldiers were captured. Retreating Iraqi forces caused huge ecological damage because they set fire to most of Kuwait's oil wells.

Other tensions in the region are caused by religious differences. There are two main forms of Islam, Sunni and Shiite. Sunnis follow 'the practice of the Prophet'. Shiites follow the teachings of the Prophet Muhammad's son-in-law, Ali.

Saddam Hussein (b.1937) is the leader of Iraq. He fought a costly war against Iran (1980–88) and invaded Kuwait in August 1990. US, British and other Middle East forces drove him out in February 1991.

▼ The US forces mounted a massive international military campaign to liberate their ally Kuwait when Iraq invaded in 1990. Preparation for the war was extensive but the actual fighting was fairly short-lived.

KEY DATES	
1948	Independent state of Israel declared; fighting with Arab neighbours erupts
1956	Suez crisis
1964	Palestinian Liberation Organization (PLO) founded in Lebanon
1967	Six Day War between Israel and Egypt
1973	Yom Kippur War in Israel
1979	Saddam Hussein rules Iraq
1979	Shah of Iran deposed
1980	Iraq invades Iran
1988	Iran–Iraq war ends
1990	Iraq invades Kuwait
1991	Iraq forced out of Kuwait

THE SCIENTIFIC REVOLUTION 1950–2000

The second half of the 20th century was a period of rapid development in science and technology. The age of the computer revolutionized people's lives.

Scientists and business people were able to develop discoveries made earlier in the century and put them to practical use. Business and industry realized that there were enormous financial benefits to be gained from working with universities and other academic institutions and important research was done through partnership between the two.

ELECTRONICS

One of the most breakthroughs invention was the silicon chip, a tiny component which could be cheaply mass-produced. It replaced old, bulky and fragile pieces of equipment, and enabled much smaller but more powerful electronic machines to be built. Microprocessors, complex circuits fitted onto a single chip, were widely used in electrical devices ranging from computers to space rockets and robots to telephones. The silicon chip influenced most people's lives in the late 20th century.

Since lasers were invented in the early 1960s, they have been used for a wide range of purposes that include eye surgery, construction work, mapping and weapons guidance systems.

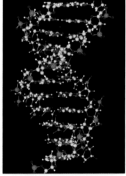

▲ The double helix (two intertwined strands) of DNA was discovered by Francis Crick and James Watson in 1953. This structure carries the blueprint for life. The discovery is helping scientists understand the causes of many diseases.

▶ By 1990, many repetitive tasks, such as the assembly-line manufacture of cars, were being carried out by computer-controlled robots. This meant that industry operated more efficiently, but it also resulted in the reduction of the human workforce.

The silicon chip microprocessor was developed in the USA in 1971 and brought about a technological revolution. The chips were 'printed' with tiny electrical circuits that enabled computers to process and store information.

THE COMPUTER AGE

The developments in electronics also generated a revolution in communications. Photocopiers and fax machines, meant that office workers could handle vast amounts of information more quickly than before. They could also communicate rapidly with other offices around the world. As electronic communications spread throughout the world, information became more freely available. By the end of the 20th century, anyone with a personal computer and a phone line could contact millions of other people around the world in an instant using the Internet.

In industry, electronics also brought about a new industrial revolution. By the 1990s, most aspects of the manufacturing process in a wide range of industries were computer controlled. Repetitive tasks on assembly lines were carried out by electronic machines known as robots. Stock control, distribution and administrative systems also came under the control of computer technology.

MEDICAL BREAKTHROUGHS

First developed in the 1960s, lasers were used in surgery to clear diseased tissue and carry out delicate eye operations.

In the 1950s, British and American scientists discovered the structure of DNA, the basic building blocks from which living cells are made. This led to the production by genetic engineering of new drugs which helped cure serious diseases. The discovery of DNA means that it will one day be possible to cure many genetic illnesses, passed down through families.

Genetic engineering also meant that the new or improved strains of plants and animals, resistant to disease, could be created in the laboratory. This technology is already helping to feed people in poorer countries. There are concerns, however, that genetically modified (GM) foods may affect human health. All GM foods must be thoroughly tested.

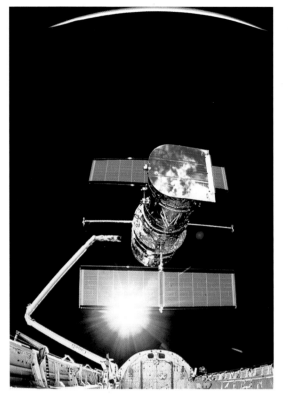

◀ The Hubble Space Telescope was launched into orbit by the US space shuttle *Discovery* in April 1990. It enabled scientists to produce images of objects billions of light years away in space.

▲ The first communication satellite was launched in 1960. The introduction, in 1964, of geosynchronous satellites, which remain over the same place on Earth, meant that any two places on Earth could be linked almost instantly.

THE WORLD WIDE WEB

The World Wide Web (www) was invented in 1990 so that users could 'surf the net' quickly. By clicking on hot-spots on the screen with the mouse, the user jumps to pages of information consisting of words and pictures located on various computers around the world. Each of these has its own hot-spots which led to further pages.

▼ Search engines greatly speed up the process of finding Web pages and specific pieces of information on the Web.

▼ People are able to view live video clips of a current US space mission from NASA.

▲ Many goods and services can be ordered and paid for over the Internet.

▶ Using email, people can send letters and pictures to one another across the world within minutes.

◀ Information on shows, films, zoos, circuses and many other forms of entertainment can be found on the Internet.

455

THE ENVIRONMENT 1950–2000

Unlike any other species on Earth, humans have the power to destroy the whole world. Only recently did people realize that the environment was threatened.

In the latter half of the 20th century, people began to realize that the Earth was in danger, threatened with pollution and over-exploitation as a result of ignorance and greed. At first only a few naturalists, such as Rachel Carson, dared to speak up. Her book *Silent Spring* caused a sensation when it was published in the 1950s. It showed how widespread the damage caused by pesticides was, and led to the banning of DDT in the USA in 1973, as well as in many other countries. Then pressure groups such as Friends of the Earth and Greenpeace also began to campaign. It slowly became clear that the environment had been seriously damaged.

The oceans in many parts of the world had been over-fished, and in many cases, scientists believed that for stocks to return to their previous levels, fishing would have to stop completely for between five and ten years. Car exhausts and factories pumped fumes into the air. Some of these gases mixed with clouds to form acid rain which kills plants. In many of the world's larger cities, like Los Angeles in California, the air quality was so polluted that a smog formed over them. Continual exposure to smog causes serious breathing problems and premature death.

On the night of March 24, 1989, the *Exxon Valdez*, a 300-metre long oil tanker, ran aground in Prince William Sound, Alaska. The ship leaked more than 35,000 tonnes of toxic petroleum over the next two days and was the biggest oil spill in American history, destroying wildlife and causing a major clean-up operation.

▼ Cities such as Sao Paulo in Brazil suffered from dangerous levels of air pollution from motor vehicles and industry.

Hundreds of oil-well fires were lit when retreating Iraqi troops left Kuwait in 1991 causing widespread pollution to the desert. It took a whole year to extinguish them all.

PROTECTING THE ENVIRONMENT

In the 1970s, British scientists working in Antarctica discovered that the ozone layer above them was becoming thinner. The ozone layer is vital to all life on Earth because it blocks much of the Sun's harmful ultraviolet radiation. It was soon learned that this protective barrier was being seriously damaged by the release of chemicals called CFCs, which were used in refrigeration and for aerosols. These chemicals have now been banned in the many countries.

By the 1980s, some governments passed laws to protect the environment, but some scientists believed that these attempts to protect our planet were too little and too late. Change was slow to take effect because at first people did not believe that the Earth was really in danger. New information was collected by scientists which proved that the threat was real. Clean (non-polluting) products started to appear but they proved expensive to buy and less profitable to produce.

It took environmental disasters such as accidents at nuclear reactors in the USA and the USSR, explosions at chemical plants in Italy and India, and oil spillage at sea, to show people that new technology could be deadly.

Public opinion gradually forced many governments to take action and to reduce pollution. Laws were passed to protect the environment and encourage conservation and recycling.

▲ Huge tracts of the tropical rainforests in South America are being destroyed so that local farmers can graze cattle.

However, in poorer countries of the world, people's only income still comes from farming or forestry which often damages the land. Their governments do not like being told by the developed world to slow growth and reduce pollution.

▲ In 1900, the world's population was around one billion. By 1990, it had risen to almost six billion. In the year 2050, almost 10 billion people will be living on the Earth.

RENEWABLE ENERGY

Most of the world's electricity is produced in power stations by burning coal, oil or gas. These fuels are known as fossil fuels and there is a limited supply of them to be taken from the Earth. Electricity made by using the force of energy from rivers (hydroelectric power), the energy from the Sun (solar energy) and from the wind (wind power), are non-polluting and are all renewable because they will not run out.

▼ Wind turbines are built on exposed sites where wind power is used to generate electricity.

▶ Solar power uses the Sun's heat to provide a clean, non-polluting source of energy.

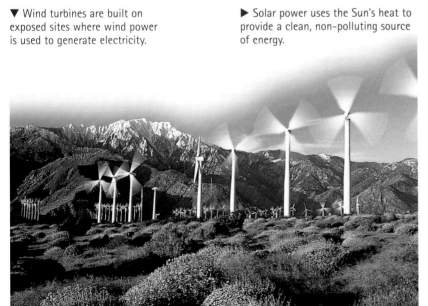

457

ASIAN ECONOMIES 1970–2000

With the help of Western aid, monetary growth in the 'tiger' economies of southeast Asia was very rapid. It soon outstripped that of the Europe and the USA.

Manufacturing was the single most important economic activity in Japan. Japanese factories used the most advanced equipment and processes available, producing high-quality goods for export to the rest of the world.

In Japan, government and business had to rebuild their economy after their defeat in World War II. They followed a different approach to China and planned a complete industrial redevelopment of their country, and rapid capitalist growth. America had occupied the Japanese islands and encouraged them to move to a democracy. They also helped Japan financially and after the war the Americans provided money at the rate of more than ten million dollars a week. The Japanese brought in industrial and land reforms and greatly improved the education system for their children. Free elections were held and women were not only allowed to vote for the first time, but some were elected to the Japanese parliament. In the 1970s and 1980s, Japan's economic growth was one of the most rapid in the world.

Along with other stock markets around the world, the Tokyo Stock Market saw panic selling in October 1987. In one day, it traded over one billion shares.

OTHER ECONOMIES

Although it took longer to get started, by the late 1970s and 1980s, South Korea's industrialization was growing at nearly ten percent every year, far more than Western countries. Again, the USA supplied aid and Japan helped as well. Hong Kong also became a major southeast Asian financial trading centre, attracting a large quantity of outside investment.

Malaysia became a major exporter of both raw materials and metals such as tin, oil and natural gas, rubber, palm oil and timber, as well as manufactured goods such as electrical machinery and semiconductors.

Singapore soon became one of the countries with a high standard of living when, in the 1960s, it began to build up its industry. Shipping took a growing part in the economy along with the establishment of extensive oil refineries. Singapore became a major exporter of petroleum products, rubber and electrical goods.

By the beginning of the 1990s, these economies gradually suffered from the downturn in world markets. Japan's export-led economy, worth more than half the region's total, had been in poor shape since 1989, and over the next ten years, its stockmarket value fell by two-thirds. This inevitably had a knock-on effect on the other countries in the region and slowed their growth dramatically.

Built as a symbol of Malaysia's once-booming economy, the twin Petronas Towers in Kuala Lumpur are the world's tallest office buildings at a height of 452 metres.

PEACEKEEPING 1950–2000

In 1945, the international community formed the United Nations to guarantee civil liberties and to work for peace and stability on a global scale.

Fifty countries formed the United Nations after the end of World War II. At the end of the century, the membership had increased to over 180.

The United Nations was formed after World War II with the intention of trying to ensure that such a war could not happen again. It was established to maintain international peace and security, to develop friendly relations among nations, to achieve international co-operation in solving economic, social and cultural problems and to encourage respect for human rights and for fundamental freedoms. Delegates from 50 nations attended what was known as the United Nations Conference on International Organization in San Francisco in April 1945. The United Nations charter was approved in June, and the organization's headquarters were located in New York.

THE SECURITY COUNCIL
Keeping international peace is the job of the UN Security Council. The permanent members are China, France, Britain, the USA and Russia; there are ten other members who are elected for two-year terms.

During the 1990s, Britain used its significant naval presence to support UN peacekeeping and humanitarian missions in many parts of the world.

WORLD PEACEKEEPING
A United Nations peacekeeping force was used for the first time during the Korean War in 1950, and they remained there until 1953, when an armistice was signed. Further deployment occurred in Egypt during the Suez Crisis in 1956 when UN forces supervized the withdrawal of invading British, French and Israeli forces.

The first large-scale UN operation in Africa went into action in 1960. Belgium had granted independence to the Republic of the Congo, now known as Zaire, but civil unrest threatened the new country. UN troops were able to provide aid as well as security. In the following years, UN peacekeeping forces were involved in many troubled areas of the world including Cyprus, Lebanon, Somalia and Rwanda.

▲ The civil war in Lebanon between Christians and a Muslim-PLO alliance in 1975–76 caused much destruction and bloodshed. United Nations forces were sent in as a peacekeeping force.

▶ During conflicts in the former Yugoslavia in the 1990s, UN peacekeeping troops were fired upon by more than one side. Here, French UN troops keep a watchful eye out for snipers in Sarajevo's notorious sniper alley.

459

WORLD TROUBLE SPOTS 1950–2000

After World War II, border disputes and wars between countries continued. Sometimes the wars involved other nations who had strategic and commercial interests.

The end of World War II did not result in peace for all the peoples of the world. Border disputes and wars between countries continued. In Korea and Vietnam, wars involved other nations, such as America, the USSR and China. In other places, the superpowers supplied arms and finance to third parties without getting involved directly. In Afghanistan, the Russians moved their own army into the country in 1979 to fight the Islamic rebels, while the United States secretly provided training, arms and money to the rebel groups.

Many parts of the world have been troubled by civil wars. Families have been divided, economies have been weakened and torn apart by famine, disease and death. These conflicts have frequently occurred because political boundaries between nations sometimes did not fit in with traditional geographical, cultural, language or religious frontiers.

▲ The Tamil Tigers are the freedom fighters who have fought for independence from Sri Lanka since 1983.

▼ Indian soldiers inspect a captured Pakistani tank after border clashes over disputed territory in Kashmir during the Indo-Pakistan conflict of 1965.

In 1995, the UN sent a peacekeeping force to Rwanda after the death of President Habyarimana led to the Hutu people murdering around half a million Tutsi people.

CONFLICT OVER KASHMIR

When the Indian sub-continent gained its independence from the British empire in 1947, the division between Pakistan and India involved the movement of millions of people. Around three and a half million Hindus and Sikhs moved from their homes in what was about to become Pakistan. At the same time, around five million Muslims moved from India to Pakistan. Such a vast disruption in so many peoples' lives caused great problems, and the ownership of the territory of Kashmir, in between the two countries, soon came to be a matter of dispute. There were numerous border skirmishes after this partition, and India managed to take over about two-thirds of the state. The dispute became of great importance to the world when it was revealed in 1998 that both countries had nuclear weapons.

THE BREAK-UP OF YUGOSLAVIA

Following the death of President Tito in 1980, Yugoslavia was soon split apart by its many different ethnic and religious peoples all demanding independence. Macedonia, Croatia, Slovenia and Bosnia–Herzegovina all declared their independence from Yugoslavia in 1991. The Serbs declared war, and fighting in Croatia lasted seven months. In Bosnia, Muslims, Croats and Serbs fought each other. Thousands of Muslims were killed by the Serbs in so-called 'ethnic cleansing'. In 1999, NATO, the Western military alliance, used military force in an attempt to protect Albanians living in Kosovo.

THE FIGHT FOR FREEDOM

Groups like the Basques in Spain, the Shan peoples in Myanmar, formerly Burma, or the Eritreans in Ethiopia felt trapped within a larger state. In Northern Ireland, the majority of the people wanted to remain part of the United Kingdom while a minority of people wanted to unify the whole island. The 'troubles', as the situation became known, have resulted in the death of thousands of people. The collapse of the USSR also resulted in a huge number of peoples having to re-establish their national identity. At the end of the 20th century, many of the world's people still sought justice and freedom.

▲ Bosnia declared independence from Yugoslavia in 1992, against the wishes of the local Serb population. A bloody civil war broke out between the many different ethnic and religious groups in the country.

◀ Soviet forces entered Afghanistan in 1979 in support of the left-wing government. During the 1980s, Islamic Mujiahideen rebels, armed by the West, fought a guerrilla campaign that forced Russian troops to withdraw in 1989, and rebels overthrew the government.

▲ Although the war between North and South Korea ended in 1953, the border between the two countries is still heavily guarded.

◀ The Kurds are a tribal people of the mountainous regions of southwest Asia. Their struggle for independence has led to bitter conflicts. Kurdish refugees, fleeing persecution from Iraq's Saddam Hussein in 1991, were not allowed entry into eastern Turkey.

SOUTH AFRICA 1990–2000

South Africa was the last bastion of imperialist, white minority rule in Africa. The release of Nelson Mandela from prison in 1990 signalled the end of apartheid.

Frederick W. de Klerk (b.1936) became president of South Africa in 1989 after P. W. Botha resigned through ill health. De Klerk worked towards ending apartheid.

▲ Nelson Rolihlahla Mandela (b.1918) shared the Nobel Peace Prize with F. W. de Klerk in 1993 for their work in ending apartheid. Following free elections in 1994, he became the first black president of South Africa.

Apartheid, the separation of people according to their colour or race, was begun by the Boers in South Africa at the beginning of the 20th century. It separated the people of South Africa into whites, black Africans and 'coloureds', people of mixed race. Asians were later added as a fourth group. The African National Congress (ANC) was formed in 1912 to fight these repressive laws.

The South African, white-dominated, government brought in a series of harsh laws to try to suppress opposition. In 1960, it made all black political parties illegal after the violent anti-apartheid riots at Sharpeville. In the mid-1970s, the government relaxed its controls a little and started to allow some unions. In the mid-1980s, the government allowed coloureds into Parliament but not black people.

The ANC and other black political parties wanted a true democracy where everyone had a vote irrespective of their colour or race. P. W. Botha, president of South Africa from 1978, was the first white leader to want reform.

As the Archbishop of Cape Town and head of the Anglican church, Desmond Tutu (b.1931) won the Nobel Peace Prize in 1984 for his fight against apartheid.

THE REFORMER

Although Botha had brought in some changes to make life fairer for blacks these had not made a radical difference. His health failed him and he resigned in 1989. A reformer, F. W. de Klerk, then became president, and in 1990, ended the ban on black people's political parties, including the ANC. In order to show he really intended change, he also had many black political prisoners released from prison. One of these was Nelson Mandela, who had been in prison since 1964. De Klerk had regular meetings with him, both while he was in prison and after his release.

▶ Under apartheid, many black South Africans were moved out of cities and forced to live in slum conditions in shanty towns on the outskirts.

THE END OF APARTHEID

Nelson Mandela became the leader of the ANC. He campaigned for the civil rights of his people, but he also argued strongly for a peaceful settlement. By working closely with de Klerk, it was possible for both white and black people to work for change. In 1992, de Klerk organized a whites-only referendum that asked whether they would like to end apartheid. Two-thirds of the votes were in favour of ending apartheid.

After a great deal of negotiation, the first free election, in which black people could also vote, was held in South Africa in April 1994. The ANC won a decisive victory and Nelson Mandela became the first black president of South Africa when de Klerk handed over power to him in May. Although the ANC now formed a government, de Klerk stayed on as one of two vice-presidents.

Although a great victory for equality had been won, the new democracy still faced enormous problems. By the end of the century there were two million children who were receiving no schooling at all. Over half of the people still lived in homes without electricity. Twelve million people had no access to a steady supply of clean drinking water. A third of the adult population was unemployed. And the great gap between the rich and the poor created a major rise in street crime.

▲ The modern city of Johannesburg is the financial centre of South Africa and lies in the area known as Witwatersrand, at the heart of the gold mining area.

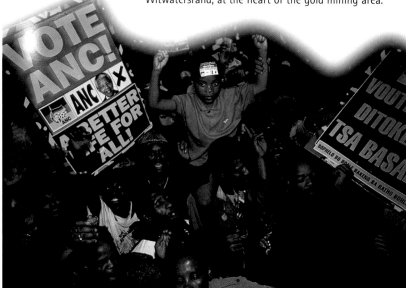

▲ Supporters of Nelson Mandela celebrate the triumph of the African National Congress after the first free elections in South Africa in 1994. The ANC were clear winners and Nelson Mandela became president.

◄ Following the end of apartheid, some South African white farmers were concerned that the huge farms that they lived on would be taken away from them by the government and given to black farmers in land redistribution.

YEAR 2000 AND BEYOND

The 20th century ended with a technological revolution yet our world is still threatened by war, poverty and human rights abuses. What does the future hold for us?

Racial harmony, tolerance, equal opportunity and individual freedom will be important factors taught to young people for achieving world peace and prosperity in the future.

The 20th century saw more change in the world than any previous century. Most of the household objects that we now use every day and take for granted did not exist a hundred years ago. The motor car was in its infancy and telephone and radio were still in the early stages of development. The televison, video recorder, credit card, computer and jet aeroplane had not yet been thought of.

At the end of the 20th century, the ability to communicate with people all over the world, thanks to the Internet and modern satellite telecommunications, brought about an explosion of information exchange. It also made it difficult for some governments to keep people in ignorance of what was happening elsewhere.

PREDICTIONS AND CONCERNS

It would have been very hard for someone living in 1900 to foretell these changes and we can only guess at our future during the coming century.

There are some things that seem likely – for example, that doctors and scientists will invent new ways of preventing and curing more diseases. Other predictions are more speculative. We would like to think that major wars will be a thing of the past, but there is no guarantee of this.

The growing population of the world is a major concern for the future. Although as a planet we grow enough food to feed everyone, millions go without because it is not distributed evenly. Most of the children in poorer countries still receive little or no education, which makes self-improvement impossible.

The environmental concerns of the latter half of the 20th century will continue to perplex governments and scientists. The Earth has finite resources that need to be carefully looked after and shared among all of its peoples.

International co-operation will be an important factor in the exploration of our resource-rich solar system. This artist's impression of a manned base on Mars shows what many people believe will be the next great space adventure. It will take an enormous amount of money and resources to accomplish, but there is good reason to believe it may happen in the first half of the 21st century.

READY
REFERENCE
40,000BC – AD2000

READY REFERENCE

ANCIENT EGYPTIAN DYNASTIES

PERIOD	DYNASTY	DATES (BC)	PRINCIPAL PHARAOHS
Early Dynastic	1–3	c. 2925–2575	Menes (Aha)
			Zoser (Djoser)
Old Kingdom	4–7/8	c. 2575–2130	Khufu (Cheops)
First Intermediate Period	9–11	c. 2130–2040	
Middle Kingdom	11–14	c. 2040–1600	Mentuhotep II
Second Intermediate Period	15–17	1630–1540	Hyksos kings rule lower Egypt
			Ahmose reunites Egypt
New Kingdom	18–20	1550–1070	Amenhotep I–III
			Thutmose I–IV
			Queen Hatshepsut
			Akhenaten (Amenhotep IV)
			Tutankhamun
			Ramesses I–XI
Third Intermediate Period	21–25	1070–656	Sheshonq I
			Rule of Nubians
Late Period	25–31	664–332	Psammatichus I
			Rule of Persians (D. 27 and 31)
			Nectanebo II
			Conquest of Alexander the Great

CHINESE DYNASTIES

DYNASTY	DATE	DETAILS
Xia	c.2200–1766BC	
Shang	1766–1122BC	
Zhou	1122–221BC	
Qin	221–206BC	Shi Huangdi, first emperor of unified China
Early Han	202BC–AD9	Emperor Wu Di also rules Korea and southern China
Hsin	AD9–25	Wang Mang takes power
Later Han	25–220	Han rule restored
The Three Kingdoms	220–280	China breaks into three kingdoms – the Wei, Shu and Wu
Western Jin	265–317	
Eastern Jin	317–420	
Southern dynasties	420–589	
Sui	589–618	China reunified
Tang	618–907	Golden age of culture; includes reign of Emperor T'ai Tsung the Great
The five dynasties and ten kingdoms	907–960	Period of civil wars
Liao	907–1125	Part of northern China ruled by Khitan Mongols
Song	960–1279	Dynasty rules parts of China only
Northern Song	960–1127	
Western Hsia	990–1227	
Chin	1115–1234	
Southern Song	1127–1279	
Yuan (Mongol)	1279–1368	All China ruled by the Mongols led by Kublai Khan
Ming	1368–1644	Re-establishment of a native Chinese dynasty
Qing (Manchu)	1644–1911	
Republic of China	1911–1949	Government set up under Sun Yat-sen, followed by disunity and the warlord era
People's Republic of China	1949–	Mao Zedong is first chairman of Communist Party

ROMAN RULERS

KINGS OF ROME

Romulus	753–716BC	Tarquinios Priscus	616–579
Numa Pompilius	716–673BC	Servius Tullius	579–534
Tullus Hostilius	673–640BC	Tarquinius Superbus	534–509
Ancus Martius	640–616BC		

THE REPUBLIC OF ROME — 509–27BC

Dictatorship of Sulla	82–78BC	Dictatorship of Julius Caesar	45–44
First Triumvirate	60–53BC	Second Triumvirate	43–27
(Julius Caesar, Pompey and Crassus)		(Octavian, Mark Anthony and Marcus	
Dictatorship of Pompey	52–47BC	Lepidus)	

EMPERORS OF THE ROMAN EMPIRE

Augustus (previously Octavian)	27BC–AD14	Gallus and Hostilianus (Volusianus)	251–253
Tiberius I	AD14–37	Aemilianus	253
Caligula (Gaius Caesar)	37–41	Valerian and Gallienus	253–260
Claudius I	41–54	Gallienus	253–268
Nero	54–68	Claudius II (Gothicus)	268–270
Galba	68–69	Quintillus	269–270
Otho	69	Aurelianus	270–275
Vitellius	69	Tacitus	275–276
Vespasian	69–79	Florianus	276
Titus	79–81	Probus	276–282
Domitian	81–96	Carus	282–283
Nerva	96–98	Carinus and Numerianus	283–284
Trajan	98–117	Diocletian (divides empire)	284–305
Hadrian	117–138	Maximilian (jointly)	286–305
Antoninus Pius	138–161	Constantius I	305–306
Marcus Aurelius	161–180	Severus	306–307
Lucius Verus (jointly)	161–169	Licinius (jointly)	308–324
Commodus	177–192	Constantine I (reunites empire)	312–337
Pertinax	193	Constantine II (jointly)	337–340
Didius Julianus	193	Constans (jointly)	337–350
Septimus Severus	193–211	Constantius II (jointly)	337–361
Caracalla	198–217	Magnentius (jointly)	350–353
Geta (jointly)	209–212	Julian (the Apostate)	361–363
Macrinus	217–218	Jovianus	363–364
Elagabulus (Heliogabalus)	218–222	Valentinian I (rules West)	364–375
Alexander Severus	222–235	Valens (rules East)	364–378
Maximinius I (the Thracian)	235–238	Gratian (rules West)	375–383
Gordian I	238	Magnus Maximus (usurper in West)	383–388
Gordian II	238	Valentinian II (rules West)	375–392
Balbinus and Pupienus Maximus	238	Eugenius (usurper in West)	392–394
Gordian III	238–244	Theodosius I (the Great)	379–395
Philip (the Arab)	244–249	(rules East, then unites East and West)	
Decius	249–251		

EMPERORS OF THE EASTERN ROMAN EMPIRE

Arcadius	395–408	Leo II	474
Theodosius II	408–450	Zeno	474–491
Marcian	450–457	Anastasius	491–518
Leo I	457–474		

EMPERORS OF THE WESTERN ROMAN EMPIRE

Honorius	395–423	Majorian	457–461
Maximus	410–411	Severus III	461–467
Constantius III	421	Anthemius	467–472
John	423–425	Olybrius	472
Valentinian III	425–455	Glycerius	473–474
Petronius Maximus	455	Julius Nepos	474–475
Avitus	455–456	Romulus Augustus	475–476

POPES

The head of the Roman Catholic Church is chosen by the cardinals of the Church. Occasionally rival popes have been elected in opposition to the chosen pope; the rivals are known as anti-popes (A.P.). There were many other popes before these, the first pope was St Peter in AD42.

Sylvester II	999	Gregory VIII	1187	Adrian VI	1522
John XVII	1003	Celestine III	1191	Clement VII	1523
John XVIII	1004	Innocent III	1198	Paul III	1534
Sergius IV	1009	Honorius III	1216	Julius III	1550
Benedict VIII	1012	Gregory IX	1227	Marcellus II	1555
Gregory (A.P.)	1012	Celestine IV	1241	Paul IV	1555
John XIX	1024	Innocent IV	1243	Pius IV	1559
Benedict IX	1032	Alexander IV	1254	St Pius V	1566
Sylvester III	1045	Urban IV	1261	Gregory XIII	1572
Benedict IX	1045	Clement IV	1265	Sixtus V	1585
Gregory VI	1045	Blessed Gregory X	1271	Urban VII	1590
Clement II	1046	Blessed Innocent V	1276	Gregory XIV	1590
Benedict IX	1047	Adrian V	1276	Innocent IX	1591
Damasus II	1048	John XXI	1276	Clement VIII	1592
St Leo IX	1049	Nicholas III	1277	Leo XI	1605
Victor II	1055	Martin IV	1281	Paul V	1605
Stephen IX (X)	1057	Honorius IV	1285	Gregory XV	1621
Benedict X (A.P.)	1058	Nicholas IV	1288	Urban VIII	1623
Nicholas II	1059	St Celestine V	1294	Innocent X	1644
Alexander II	1061	Boniface VIII	1294	Alexander VII	1655
Honorius II (A.P.)	1061	Blessed Benedict XI	1303	Clement IX	1667
St Gregory VII	1073	Clement V	1305	Clement X	1670
Clement III (A.P.)	1080	John XXII	1316	Blessed Innocent XI	1676
Blessed Victor III	1087	Nicholas V (A.P.)	1328	Alexander VIII	1689
Blessed Urban II	1088	Benedict XII	1334	Innocent XII	1691
Paschal II	1099	Clement VI	1342	Clement XI	1700
Theodorie (A.P.)	1100	Innocent VI	1352	Innocent XIII	1721
Albert (A.P.)	1102	Blessed Urban V	1362	Benedict XIII	1724
Sylvester IV (A.P.)	1105	Gregory XI	1370	Clement XII	1730
Gelasius II	1118	Urban VI	1378	Benedict XIV	1740
Gregory VIII (A.P.)	1118	Clement VII (A.P.)	1378	Clement XIII	1758
Callistus II	1119	Boniface IX	1389	Clement XIV	1769
Honorius II	1124	Benedict XIII (A.P.)	1394	Pius VI	1775
Celestine II (A.P.)	1124	Innocent VII	1404	Pius VII	1800
Innocent II	1130	Gregory XII	1406	Leo XII	1823
Anacletus II (A.P.)	1130	Alexander V (A.P.)	1409	Pius VIII	1829
Victor IV (A.P.)	1138	John XXIII	1410	Gregory XVI	1831
Celestine II	1143	Martin V	1417	Pius IX	1846
Lucius II	1144	Eugene IV	1431	Leo XIII	1878
Blessed Eugene III	1145	Felix V (A.P.)	1439	St Pius X	1903
Anastasius IV	1153	Nicholas V	1447	Benedict XV	1914
Adrian IV	1154	Callistus III	1455	Pius XI	1922
Alexander III	1159	Pius II	1458	Pius XII	1939
Victor IV (A.P.)	1159	Paul II	1464	John XXIII	1958
Paschal III (A.P.)	1164	Sixtus IV	1471	Paul VI	1963
Callistus III (A.P.)	1168	Innocent VIII	1484	John Paul I	1978
Innocent III (A.P.)	1179	Alexander VI	1492	John Paul II	1978
Lucius III	1181	Pius III	1503		
Urban III	1185	Julius II	1503		
Clement III	1187	Leo X	1513		

RULERS OF ENGLAND

SAXONS

Egbert	829–839	Edred	946–955
Ethelwulf	839–858	Edwy	955–959
Ethelbald	858–860	Edgar	959–975
Ethelbert	860–865	Edward the Martyr	975–978
Ethelred I	865–871	Ethelred II, the Unready	978–1016
Alfred the Great	871–899	Sweyn Forkbeard	1013–1014
Edward the Elder	899–924	Ethelred II, the Unready (restored)	1014–1016
Athelstan	924–939	Edmund Ironside	1016
Edmund	939–946		

DANES

Canute	1016–1035	Harthacanute	1040–1042
Harold I Harefoot	1035–1040		

SAXONS

Edward the Confessor	1042–1066	Harold II	1066

HOUSE OF NORMANDY

William I, the Conqueror	1066–1087	Henry I	1100–1135
William II	1087–1100	Stephen	1135–1154

HOUSE OF PLANTAGENET

Henry II	1154–1189	Edward I	1272–1307
Richard I, the Lionheart	1189–1199	Edward II	1307–1327
John	1199–1216	Edward III	1327–1377
Henry III	1216–1272	Richard II	1377–1399

HOUSE OF LANCASTER

Henry IV	1399–1413	Henry VI	1422–1461
Henry V	1413–1422		

HOUSE OF YORK

Edward IV	1461–1483	Richard III	1483–1485
Edward V	1483		

HOUSE OF TUDOR

Henry VII	1485–1509	Mary I	1553–1558
Henry VIII	1509–1547	Elizabeth I	1558–1603
Edward VI	1547–1553		

RULERS OF SCOTLAND

Malcolm II	1005–1034	Malcolm IV	1153–1165
Duncan I	1034–1040	William the Lion	1165–1214
Macbeth (usurper)	1040–1057	Alexander II	1214–1249
Malcolm III (Cranmore)	1057–1093	Alexander III	1249–1286
Donald Bane	1093–1094	Margaret of Norway	1286–1290
Duncan II	1094	(Interregnum	1290–1291)
Donald Bane (restored)	1094–1097	John Balliol	1292–1296
Edgar	1097–1107	(Interregnum	1296–1306)
Alexander I	1107–1124	Robert I, the Bruce	1306–1329
David I	1124–1153	David II	1329–1371

HOUSE OF STUART

		James III	1460–1488
Robert II	1371–1390	James IV	1488–1513
Robert III	1390–1406	James V	1513–1542
James I	1406–1437	Mary, Queen of Scots	1542–1567
James II	1437–1460	James VI (I of Great Britain)	1567–1625

RULERS OF ENGLAND AND SCOTLAND

HOUSE OF STUART

James I	1603–1625	Charles I	1625–1649

COMMONWEALTH	**1649–1653**
PROTECTORATE	**1653–1660**

Oliver Cromwell	1653–1658	Richard Cromwell	1658–1659

HOUSE OF STUART

Charles II	1660–1685	William III (jointly)	1689–1702
James II	1685–1688	Anne	1702–1714
Mary II (jointly)	1689–1694		

RULERS OF GREAT BRITAIN

HOUSE OF HANOVER

George I	1714–1727	George IV	1820–1830
George II	1727–1760	William IV	1830–1837
George III	1760–1820	Victoria	1837–1901

HOUSE OF SAXE–COBURG

Edward VII	1901–1910

HOUSE OF WINDSOR

George V	1910–1936	George VI	1936–1952
Edward VIII	1936	Elizabeth II	1952–

PRIME MINISTERS OF GREAT BRITAIN

	IN OFFICE	PARTY
Sir Robert Walpole	1721–1742	Whig
Earl of Wilmington	1742–1743	Whig
Henry Pelham	1743–1754	Whig
Duke of Newcastle	1754–1756	Whig
Duke of Devonshire	1756–1757	Whig
Duke of Newcastle	1757–1762	Whig
Earl of Bute	1762–1763	Tory
George Grenville	1763–1765	Whig
Marquess of Rockingham	1765–1766	Whig
William Pitt the Elder (Earl of Chatham)	1766–1768	Whig
Duke of Grafton	1768–1770	Whig
Lord North	1770–1782	Tory
Marquess of Rockingham	1782	Whig
Earl of Shelburne	1782–1783	Whig
Duke of Portland	1783	Coalition
William Pitt the Younger	1783–1801	Tory
Henry Addington	1801–1804	Tory
William Pitt the Younger	1804–1806	Tory
Lord Grenville	1806–1807	Whig
Duke of Portland	1807–1809	Tory
Spencer Perceval	1809–1812	Tory
Earl of Liverpool	1812–1827	Tory
George Canning	1827	Tory
Viscount Goderich	1827–1828	Tory
Duke of Wellington	1828–1830	Tory
Earl Grey	1830–1834	Whig
Viscount Melbourne	1834	Whig
Sir Robert Peel	1834–1835	Tory
Viscount Melbourne	1835–1841	Whig

Sir Robert Peel	1841–1846	Tory
Lord John Russell	1846–1852	Whig
Earl of Derby	1852	Tory
Earl of Aberdeen	1852–1855	Peelite
Viscount Palmerston	1855–1858	Liberal
Earl of Derby	1858–1859	Conservative
Viscount Palmerston	1859–1865	Liberal
Earl Russell	1865–1866	Liberal
Earl of Derby	1866–1868	Conservative
Benjamin Disraeli	1868	Conservative
William Gladstone	1868–1874	Liberal
Benjamin Disraeli	1874–1880	Conservative
William Gladstone	1880–1885	Liberal
Marquess of Salisbury	1885–1886	Conservative
William Gladstone	1886	Liberal
Marquess of Salisbury	1886–1892	Conservative
William Gladstone	1892–1894	Liberal
Earl of Rosebery	1894–1895	Liberal
Marquess of Salisbury	1895–1902	Conservative
Arthur Balfour	1902–1905	Conservative
Sir Henry Campbell-Bannerman	1905–1908	Liberal
Herbert Asquith	1908–1915	Liberal
Herbert Asquith	1915–1916	Coalition
David Lloyd George	1916–1922	Coalition
Andrew Bonar Law	1922–1923	Conservative
Stanley Baldwin	1923–1924	Conservative
James Ramsay MacDonald	1924	Labour
Stanley Baldwin	1924–1929	Conservative
James Ramsay MacDonald	1929–1931	Labour
James Ramsay MacDonald	1931–1935	National Coalition
Stanley Baldwin	1935–1937	National Coalition
Neville Chamberlain	1937–1940	National Coalition
Winston Churchill	1940–1945	Coalition
Winston Churchill	1945	Conservative
Clement Atlee	1945–1951	Labour
Sir Winston Churchill	1951–1955	Conservative
Sir Anthony Eden	1955–1957	Conservative
Harold Macmillan	1957–1963	Conservative
Sir Alec Douglas-Home	1963–1964	Conservative
Harold Wilson	1964–1970	Labour
Edward Heath	1970–1974	Conservative
Harold Wilson	1974–1976	Labour
James Callaghan	1976–1979	Labour
Margaret Thatcher	1979–1990	Conservative
John Major	1990–1997	Conservative
Tony Blair	1997–	Labour

HOLY ROMAN EMPERORS

Dates given are period of reign

Charlemagne	800–814	Louis II	855–875
Louis I (the Pious)	814–840	Charles II	875–877
Lothair I	843–855	Charles III	881-891

HOUSE OF SPOLETO

Guy	891–894	Lambert	894–898

CAROLINGIAN DYNASTY

Arnulf	896–899	Louis III	901–905

HOUSE OF FRANCONIA

Conrad I	911–918

CAROLINGIAN DYNASTY

Berengar	915–924		

SAXON DYNASTY

Henry I	919–936	Otto III	983–1002
Otto I, the Great	936–973	Henry II	1002–1024
Otto II	973–983		

FRANCONIAN DYNASTY

Conrad II	1024–1039	Henry V	1106–1125
Henry III	1039–1056	Lothair III, Duke of Saxony	1125–1137
Henry IV	1056–1106		

HOHENSTAUFEN DYNASTY

Conrad III	1138–1152	Otto IV of Brunswick	1198–1214
Frederick I, Barbarossa	1152–1190	Frederick II	1212–1250
Henry VI	1190–1197	Conrad IV	1250–1254
Philip of Swabia	1197–1208		

INTERREGNUM

Electors gain power	1254–1273		

TRANSITION PERIOD

Rudolf I of Habsburg	1273–1292	Frederick of Austria (co-regent)	1314–1326
Adolf of Nassau	1292–1298	Charles IV, of Luxembourg	1347–1378
Albert I, King of Germany	1298–1308	Wenceslas of Luxembourg	1378–1400
Henry VII of Luxembourg	1308–1314	Rupert, Duke of Palatine	1400–1410
Louis IV of Bavaria (co-regent)	1314–1347	Sigismund of Luxembourg	1410–1437

HABSBURG DYNASTY

Albert II	1437–1439	Leopold I	1658–1705
Frederick III	1452–1493	Joseph I	1705–1711
Maximilian I	1493–1519	Charles VI	1711–1740
Charles V, King of Spain	1519–1556	War of the Austrian Succession	1740–1748
Ferdinand I	1558–1564	Charles VII of Bavaria	1742–1745
Maximilian II	1564–1576	Francis I of Lorraine	1745–1765
Rudolf II	1576–1612	Joseph II	1765–1790
Matthias	1612–1619	Leopold II	1790–1792
Ferdinand II	1619–1637	Francis II	1792–1806
Ferdinand III	1637–1657		

HABSBURG EMPERORS OF AUSTRIA

Francis II	1804–1835	Francis Joseph	1848–1916
Ferdinand	1835–1848	Charles	1916–1918

HOHENZOLLERN EMPERORS OF GERMANY

William I (of Prussia)	1871–1888	William II	1888–1918
Frederick III	1888		

RULERS OF GERMANY

WEIMAR REPUBLIC

Friedrich Ebert	1919–1925	Paul von Hindenburg	1925–1934

THIRD REICH

Adolf Hitler	1934–1945		

POST WORLD WAR II

Germany under Allied control	1945–1949		

CHANCELLORS OF THE FEDERAL REPUBLIC OF GERMANY (WEST GERMANY)

Konrad Adenauer	1949–1963	Willy Brandt	1969–1974
Dr Ludwig Erhard	1963–1966	Helmut Schmidt	1974–1982
Kurt George Kiesinger	1966–1969	Helmut Kohl	1982–1990

CHAIRMEN OF THE DEMOCRATIC REPUBLIC OF GERMANY (EAST GERMANY)

Walter Ulbricht	1949–1971	Egon Krenz	1989–1990
Erich Honecker	1971–1989		

CHANCELLORS OF UNITED GERMANY

Helmut Kohl	1990–1998	Gerhard Schroder	1998–

RULERS OF FRANCE

THE CAROLINGIANS

Charles II, the Bald	843–877	Robert	922–923
Louis II	877–879	Rudolph	923–936
Louis III	879–882	Louis IV	936–954
Charles III	884–887	Lothair	954–986
Eudes	888–898	Louis V	986–987
Charles III	898–922		

THE CAPETS

Hugh Capet	987–996	Louis VIII	1223–1226
Robert II, the Pious	996–1031	Louis IX	1226–1270
Henry I	1031–1060	Philip III	1270–1285
Philip I	1060–1108	Philip IV	1285–1314
Louis VI	1108–1137	Louis X	1314–1316
Louis VII	1137–1180	Philip V	1316–1322
Philip II	1180–1223	Charles IV	1322–1328

HOUSE OF VALOIS

Philip VI	1328–1350	Louis XII	1498–1515
John II	1350–1364	Francis I	1515–1547
Charles V	1364–1380	Henry II	1547–1559
Charles VI	1380–1422	Francis II	1559–1560
Charles VII	1422–1461	Charles IX	1560–1574
Louis XI	1461–1483	Henry III	1574–1589
Charles VIII	1483–1498		

HOUSE OF BOURBON

Henry IV, of Navarre	1589–1610	Louis XV	1715–1774
Louis XIII	1610–1643	Louis XVI	1774–1793
Louis XIV	1643–1715	Louis XVII	1793–1795

THE FIRST REPUBLIC AND FIRST EMPIRE

Napoleon Bonaparte (first consul)	1799–1804	Napoleon I (emperor)	1804–1814

RESTORATION OF MONARCHY

Louis XVIII	1814–1824	Louis-Philippe	1830–1848
Charles X	1824–1830		

SECOND REPUBLIC

Louis Napoleon Bonaparte (president)	1848–1852	Napoleon III (emperor)	1852–1870

THIRD REPUBLIC

Louis Adolphe Thiers	1871–1873	Paul Deschanel	1920
Marshal Patrice de MacMahon	1873–1879	Alexander Millerand	1920–1924
Paul Grévy	1879–1887	Gaston Doumergue	1924–1931
Marie Carnot	1887–1894	Paul Doumer	1931–1932
Jean Casimir-Périer	1894–1895	Albert Lebrun	1932–1940
François Faure	1895–1899	Vichy government (under Germans)	1940–1944
Émile Loubet	1899–1906		
Armand C. Fallières	1906–1913	Provisional government	1944–1946
Raymond Poincaré	1913–1920		

FOURTH REPUBLIC

Vincent Auriol	1947–1954	René Coty	1954–1959

FIFTH REPUBLIC

Charles de Gaulle	1959–1969	Valéry Giscard d'Estaing	1974–1981
Georges Pompidou	1969–1974	François Mitterrand	1981–1995
		Jacques Chirac	1995–

RULERS OF SPAIN

HABSBURG DYNASTY

Charles I (V of Germany)	1516–1556	Philip IV	1621–1665
Philip II	1556–1598	Charles II	1665–1700
Philip III	1598–1621		

BOURBON DYNASTY

Philip V	1700–1724	Charles IV	1788–1808
Louis I	1724	Ferdinand VII	1808
Philip V (restored)	1724–1746	Joseph Bonaparte	1808–1814
Ferdinand VI	1746–1759	Ferdinand VII	1814–1833
Charles III	1759–1788	Isabella II	1833–1868

OTHER MONARCHS

Amadeus of Savoy	1870–1873

FIRST REPUBLIC

1873–1874

RESTORATION OF MONARCHY

Alfonso XII	1874–1885	Alfonso XIII	1886–1931
General Miguel Primo de Rivera (dictator)	1923–1930		

SECOND REPUBLIC

Niceto Alcalá Zamora	1931–1936	General Francisco Franco	1939–1975
Manuel Azaña	1936–1939		

RESTORATION OF MONARCHY

Juan Carlos	1975–

PRIME MINISTERS

Admiral Luis Blanco	1973	Felipe González Márquez	1982–1996
Carlos Navarro	1973–1976	Jose Maria Aznar	1996–
Adolfo Suárez	1976–1982		

PERIODS OF JAPAN

Yamato	c.300–592	
Asaka	592–710	Empress Suiko (592–628)
		Emperor Temmu (673–686)
Nara	710–794	Emperor Kammu (781–806)
Heian	794–1185	Japan ruled from Heian (now called Kyoto)
Fujiwara	858–1160	Fujiwara clan rules
Taira	1159–1185	Taira clan take control

Kamakura	1185–1333	Minamoto Yoritomo defeats Taira clan; in 1192 he becomes shogun
Namboku	1334–1392	End of shogun rule in 1333; Emperor Godaigo rules alone 1333–1339; imperial line splits into northern and southern courts
Ashikaga	1338–1573	Ashikaga Takauji becomes shogun in 1338
Muromachi	1392–1573	Two rival courts are unified
Sengoku	1467–1600	Emperor Gonara (1527–1557)
Momoyama	1573–1603	Oda Nobunaga, a daimyo (baron), deposes the shogun and becomes dictator to 1582
Edo	1603–1867	Ieyasu Tokugawa becomes shogun in 1603; Tokugawa shoguns rule until 1867
Meiji	1868–1912	Emperor Mutsuhito, Meiji Restoration; he ends the shogunate and modernizes Japan
Taisho	1912–1926	Emperor Yoshihito
Showa	1926–1989	Emperor Hirohito
Heisei	1989–	Emperor Akihito

TSARS OF RUSSIA

Ivan III, the Great, ruler of Russia	1462–1505	Catherine I	1725–1727
Vasili, ruler of Russia	1505–1533	Peter II	1727–1730
Ivan IV, the Terrible, first tsar	1533–1584	Anna	1730–1740
Fyodor I	1584–1598	Ivan VI	1740–1741
Boris Godunov	1598–1605	Elizabeth	1741–1762
Fyodor II	1605	Peter III	1762
Demetrius	1605–1606	Catherine II, the Great	1762–1796
Basil (IV) Shuiski	1606–1610	Paul I	1796–1801
(Interregnum	1610–1613)	Alexander I	1801–1825
Michael Romanov	1613–1645	Nicholas I	1825–1855
Alexis	1645–1676	Alexander II	1855–1881
Fyodor III	1676–1682	Alexander III	1881–1894
Ivan V and Peter I, the Great, joint rulers	1682–1689	Nicholas II	1894–1917
Peter I	1689–1725		

EFFECTIVE RULERS OF THE UNION OF SOVIET SOCIALIST REPUBLICS

Vladimir Lenin	1917–1924	Leonid Brezhnev	1964–1982
Joseph Stalin	1924–1953	Yuri Andropov	1982–1984
Georgy Malenkov	1953	Konstantin Chernenko	1984–1985
Nikita Khrushchev	1953–1964	Mikhail Gorbachev	1985–1991

PRESIDENTS OF RUSSIA

Boris Yeltsin	1991–

PRESIDENTS OF THE UNITED STATES OF AMERICA

George Washington	1789–1797	None
John Adams	1797–1801	Federalist
Thomas Jefferson	1801–1809	Democratic-Republican
James Madison	1809–1817	Democratic-Republican
James Monroe	1817–1825	Democratic-Republican
John Quincy Adams	1825–1829	Democratic-Republican
Andrew Jackson	1829–1837	Democrat
Martin Van Buren	1837–1841	Democrat
William H. Harrison	1841	Whig
John Tyler	1841–1845	Whig
James K. Polk	1845–1849	Democrat
Zachary Taylor	1849–1850	Whig
Millard Fillmore	1850–1853	Whig
Franklin Pierce	1853–1857	Democrat
James Buchanan	1857–1861	Democrat
Abraham Lincoln	1861–1865	Republican
Andrew Johnson	1865–1869	National Union

Ulysses S. Grant	1869–1877		Republican
Rutherford B. Hayes	1877–1881		Republican
James Garfield	1881		Republican
Chester Arthur	1881–1885		Republican
Grover Cleveland	1885–1889		Democrat
Benjamin Harrison	1889–1893		Republican
Grover Cleveland	1893–1897		Democrat
William McKinley	1897–1901		Republican
Theodore Roosevelt	1901–1909		Republican
William Taft	1909–1913		Republican
Woodrow Wilson	1913–1921		Democrat
Warren Harding	1921–1923		Republican
Calvin Coolidge	1923–1929		Republican
Herbert Hoover	1929–1933		Republican
Franklin D. Roosevelt	1933–1945		Democrat
Harry S. Truman	1945–1953		Democrat
Dwight Eisenhower	1953–1961		Republican
John F. Kennedy	1961–1963		Democrat
Lyndon Johnson	1963–1969		Democrat
Richard Nixon	1969–1974		Republican
Gerald Ford	1974–1977		Republican
Jimmy Carter	1977–1981		Democrat
Ronald Reagan	1981–1989		Republican
George Bush	1989–1993		Republican
Bill Clinton	1993–		Democrat

PRIME MINISTERS OF CANADA

Sir John Macdonald	1867–1873	Richard Bennett	1930–1935
Alexander Mackenzie	1873–1878	William King	1935–1948
Sir John Macdonald	1878–1891	Louis St Laurent	1948–1957
Sir John Abbott	1891–1892	John Diefenbaker	1957–1963
Sir John Thompson	1892–1894	Lester Pearson	1963–1968
Sir Mackenzie Bowell	1894–1896	Pierre Trudeau	1968–1979
Sir Charles Tupper	1896	Charles (Joe) Clark	1979–1980
Sir Wilfrid Laurier	1896–1911	Pierre Trudeau	1980–1984
Sir Robert Borden	1911–1920	John Turner	1984
Arthur Meighen	1920–1921	Brian Mulroney	1984–1993
William King	1921–1926	Kim Campbell	1993
Arthur Meighen	1926	Jean Chrétian	1993–
William King	1926–1930		

PRIME MINISTERS OF AUSTRALIA

Australia established as a Commonwealth 1901

Sir Edmund Barton	1901–1903	Sir Robert Menzies	1939–1941
Alfred Deakin	1903–1904	Sir Arthur Fadden	1941
John Watson	1904	John Curtin	1941–1945
Sir George Reid	1904–1905	Francis Forde	1945
Alfred Deakin	1905–1908	Joseph Chifley	1945–1949
Andrew Fisher	1908–1909	Sir Robert Menzies	1949–1966
Alfred Deakin	1909–1910	Harold Holt	1966–1967
Andrew Fisher	1910–1913	Sir John McEwen	1967–1968
Sir Joseph Cook	1913–1914	John Gorton	1968–1971
Andrew Fisher	1914–1915	William McMahon	1971–1972
William Hughes	1915–1923	Edward Gough Whitlam	1972–1975
Stanley Bruce	1923–1929	John Fraser	1975–1983
James Scullin	1929–1932	Robert Hawke	1983–1991
Joseph Lyons	1932–1939	Paul Keating	1991–1996
Sir Earle Page	1939	John Howard	1996–

PRIME MINISTERS OF NEW ZEALAND

Sir Joseph Ward	1906–1912	Sir Walter Nash	1957–1960
Thomas MacKenzie	1912–1915	Keith Holyoake	1960–1972
William Massey	1915–1925	Sir John Marshall	1972
Sir Francis Bell	1925	Norman Kirk	1972–1974
Joseph Coates	1925–1928	Hugh Watt	1974
Sir Joseph Ward	1928–1930	Wallace (Bill) Rowling	1974–1975
George Forbes	1930–1935	Robert Muldoon	1975–1984
Michael Savage	1935–1940	David Lange	1984–1989
Peter Fraser	1940–1949	Geoffrey Palmer	1989–1990
Sir Sidney Holland	1949–1957	Michael Moore	1990
Keith Holyoake	1957	James Bolger	1990–1997
		Jenny Shipley	1997–

PRESIDENTS OF THE REPUBLIC OF ITALY

Alcide de Gasperi (acting head of state)	1946	Giovanni Leone	1971–1978
Enrico de Nicola (provisional president)	1946–1948	Amintore Fanfani	1978
Luigi Einaudi	1948–1955	Alessandro Pemini	1978–1985
Giovanni Gronchi	1955–1962	Francesco Cossiga	1985–1992
Antonio Segni	1962–1964	Oscar Luigi Scalfaro	1992–
Giuseppe Saragat	1964–1971		

PRIME MINISTERS

Alcide de Gasperi	1946–1953	Mariano Rumor	1973–1974
Guiseppe Pella	1953–1954	Aldo Moro	1974–1976
Amintore Fanfani	1954	Giulio Andreotti	1976–1979
Mario Scelba	1954–1955	Francesco Cossiga	1979–1980
Antonio Segni	1955–1957	Arnaldo Forlani	1980–1981
Adone Zoli	1957–1958	Giovanni Spadolini	1981–1982
Amintore Fanfani	1958–1959	Armintore Fanfani	1982–1983
Antonio Segni	1959–1960	Bettino Craxi	1983–1987
Fernando Tambroni	1960	Giovanni Goria	1987–1988
Amintore Fanfani	1960–1963	Luigi Ciriaco de Mita	1988–1989
Giovanni Leone	1963	Giulio Andreotti	1989–1993
Aldo Moro	1963–1968	Carlo Azegho Ciampi	1993–1994
Giovanni Leone	1968	Silvio Berlusconi	1994–1995
Mariano Rumor	1968–1970	Lamberto Dini	1995–1996
Emilio Colombo	1970–1972	Romano Prodi	1996–1998
Giulio Andreotti	1972–1973	Massimo D'Alema	1998–

PRESIDENTS OF REPUBLIC OF INDIA

Dr Rajendra Prasad	1949–1962	Neelam Reddy	1977–1982
Dr Sarvapalli Radhakrishnan	1962–1967	Giani Zail Singh	1982–1987
Dr Zahir Hussain	1967–1969	Ramaswamy Venkataraman	1987–1992
Varahgiri Giri	1969–1974	Shankar Dayal Sharma	1992–1997
Fakhruddin Ahmed	1974–1977	K. R. Narayanan	1997–
Basappa Jatti	1977		

PRIME MINISTERS

Jawaharlal Nehru	1947–1964	Rajiv Gandhi	1984–1989
Gulzarilal Nanda	1964	V. P. Singh	1989–1990
Lal Shastri	1964–1966	Chandra Shekhar	1990–1991
Gulzarilal Nanda	1966	P. V. Narasimha Rao	1991–1996
Indira Gandhi	1966–1977	Atal Bihari Vajpayee	1996
Shri Desai	1977–1979	H. D. Deve Gowda	1996–1997
Charan Singh	1979–1980	I. K. Gujral	1997
Indira Gandhi	1980–1984	Atal Bihari Vajpayee	1997–

MAJOR WARS

DATE	NAME OF WAR	WARRING PARTIES
c. 1250 BC	Trojan wars	Myceneans v. Trojans
431–404 BC	Peloponnesian War	Athens v. Sparta
264–241 BC	First Punic War	
218–201 BC	Second Punic War	Rome v. Carthage
149–146 BC	Third Punic War	
1096–1099	First Crusade	
1147–1149	Second Crusade	
1189–1192	Third Crusade	Saracens v. Christians over Palestine
1202–1204	Fourth Crusade	
1337–1453	Hundred Years War	England v. France
1455–1485	Wars of the Roses	House of York v. House of Lancaster
1562–1598	French Wars of Religion	Huguenots v. Catholics
1642–1648	English Civil War	Cavaliers v. Roundheads
1618–1648	Thirty Years War	Catholic League (Germany, Austria, Spain) v. Denmark, Sweden, France
1689–1697	War of League of Augsburg	France v. the League, England and the Netherlands
1700	Great Northern War	Sweden v. Russia, Denmark, Poland, Holland
1701–1713	War of Spanish Succession	Spain, France and Bavaria v. England, Holland, Austrian empire and Portugal
1730–1738	War of Polish Succession	Russia, Poland v. France
1740–1748	War of Austrian Succession	Austria, Britain v. Prussia, Bavaria, France, Spain
1756–1763	Seven Years War	Britain and Prussia v. France, Austria and Russia
1775–1783	American Revolutionary War	American colonies v. Britain
1793–1815	Napoleonic wars	France v. Britain, Austria, Sweden, Russia and Prussia
1821–1829	Greek War of Independence	Greece v. Ottoman Turkey
1846–1848	Mexican-American War	Mexico v. USA
1854–1856	Crimean War	Russia v. Britain, France and Turkey
1859	War for Italian Independence	France, Piedmont-Sardinia v. Austria
1861–1865	American Civil War	Confederates v. Unionists
1866	Austro-Prussian War	Prussia v. Austria
1870	Franco-Prussian War	France v. Prussia
1894–1895	Chinese-Japanese War	China v. Japan
1899–1902	Boer War	Britain v. Boers (Dutch) in South Africa
1904–1905	Russo-Japanese War	Russia v. Japan
1914–1918	World War I	Germany and Austria-Hungary v. France, Russia, Britain and other nations
1918–1921	Russian Civil War	Bolsheviks v. White Russians
1931–1933	Chinese-Japanese War	Japan v. China
1936–1939	Spanish Civil War	Nationalists (Franco) v. Republicans
1939–1945	World War II	Britain, France, USSR, USA and other nations v. Germany, Italy and Japan
1950–1953	Korean War	North Korea v. South Korea
1967	Six-Day War	Israel v. Arab states
1964–1973	Vietnam War	North Vietnam v. South Vietnam and USA
1980–1988	Iran-Iraq War	Iran v. Iraq
1982	Falklands War	United Kingdom v. Argentina
1991	Gulf War	Iraq v. combined international forces

INDEX

483

484

485

486

ACKNOWLEDGEMENTS
The publishers wish to thank the following for their contributions to this book:

Photographs
(*t* = top; *b* = bottom; *m* = middle; *l* = left; *r* = right)

Page i *bl* ET Archive, *ml* Bridgeman Art Library; iii *mtl* Werner Forman Archive, *m* ET Archive; vi-vii Gavin Hellier/Robert Harding Picture Library; viii *bl* ET Archive; 1 *m* ET Archive; 2 Robert Harding Picture Library; 14 ET Archive; 15 Ancient Art & Architecture Collection Ltd; 16 AKG; 17 *t* ET Archive, *ml* AKG; 18 ET Archive; 19 ET Archive; 20 *tl* ET Archive, *bl* ET Archive, *br* ET Archive; 21 ET Archive; 25 Ancient Art & Architecture Collection Ltd; 28 Ancient Art & Architecture Collection Ltd; 29 Ancient Art & Architecture Collection Ltd; 30 ET Archive; 32 ET Archive; 34 AKG; 35 ET Archive; 36 ET Archive; 39 ET Archive; 40 *t* ET Archive, *b* ET Archive; 42 AKG; 43 *m* ET Archive, *b* ET Archive; 45 Mick Sharp; 48 Roy Rainford/Robert Harding Picture Library; 56 ET Archive; 57 Robert Harding Picture Library Ltd; 61 *t* Ronald Sheridan/Ancient Art & Architecture Collection Ltd, *b* Ronald Sheridan/Ancient Art & Architecture Collection Ltd; 73 Robert Harding Picture Library; 76 Robert Harding Picture Library; 78 Richard Ashworth/Robert Harding Picture Library; 79 Richard Ashworth/Robert Harding Picture Library; 81 ET Archive; 83 *t* ET Archive, *b* ET Archive; 85 Ancient Art & Architecture Collection Ltd; 93 *tl* ET Archive, *tr* G&P Corrigan/Robert Harding Picture Library; 96 Robert Frerck/Robert Harding Picture Library; 97 Bridgeman Art Library; 100 Bridgeman Art Library; 101 *t* ET Archive, *b* ET Archive; 103 ET Archive; 107 ET Archive; 108 ET Archive; 109 *t* ET Archive, *bl* Bridgeman Art Library, *br* AKG; 111 Robert Harding Picture Library/James Gritz; 113 *tl* Ancient Art & Architecture Collection, *tr* Bridgeman Art Library, *b* Bridgeman Art Library; 114 ET Archive; 115 The Bridgeman Art Library; 118 Ancient Art & Architecture Collection/C.Blankenship; 119 R. Sheridan/Ancient Art & Architecture Collection; 120 *mr* R. Sheridan/Ancient Art & Architecture Collection; 121 *t* ET Archive, *b* ET Archive; 125 AKG; 126 *l* Bridgeman Art Library, *r* AKG; 127 *t* AKG, *m* Bridgeman Art Library; 129 *t* Robert Harding Picture Library, *b* Robert Harding Picture Library; 132 Bridgeman Art Library; 135 *t* R. Sheridan/Ancient Art & Architecture Collection, *m* Ancient Art & Architecture Collection; 136 *t* ET Archive, *b* ET Archive; 137 *tl* ET Archive, *tr* ET Archive; 139 *tl* ET Archive, *tr* ET Archive; 141 ET Archive; 143 ET Archive; 144 ET Archive; 152 ET Archive; 154 ET Archive; 155 ET Archive; 160 ET Archive; 161 *t* ET Archive, *b* ET Archive; 162 ET Archive; 163 ET Archive; 164 *m* ET Archive, *b* ET Archive; 165 Robert Harding Picture Library/S. Sassoon; 167 Robert Harding Picture Library/Geoff Renner; 169 Robert Harding Picture Library; 176 ET Archive; 180 *t* ET Archive; 181 *m* ET Archive, *b* ET Archive; 183 *t* ET Archive, *b* Robert Harding Associates; 184 Robert Harding Picture Library; 185 A. Barrington/Ancient Art & Architecture Collection; 186 *t* ET Archive, *b* ET Archive; 187 Robert Harding Picture Library; 189 Robert Harding Picture Library; 192 ET Archive; 201 *tl* ET Archive, *tr* ET Archive, *b* ET Archive; 202 ET Archive; 204 Bridgeman Art Library; 205 ET Archive; 208 *tl* Ancient Art & Architecture Collection Ltd, *b* Werner Forman Archive; 209 Ancient Art & Architecture Collection Ltd; 212 *tl* Werner Forman Archive, *tr* Werner Forman Archive, *bl* Werner Forman Archive; 213 Bridgeman Art Library; 215 Bridgeman Art Library; 218 Bridgeman Art Library; 227 *t* Ancient Art & Architecture Collection Ltd, *b* Bridgeman Art Library; 228 Bridgeman Art Library; 229 *t* AKG, *b* AKG; 234 *bl* Bridgeman Art Library, *br* Ancient Art & Architecture Collection Ltd; 235 ET Archive; 238 ET Archive; 239 ET Archive; 240 Margaret Collier/Robert Harding Picture Library; 243 *mr* ET Archive, *br* ET Archive; 244 Werner Forman Archive; 245 Werner Forman Archive; 247 Bridgeman Art Library; 250 *l* ET Archive, *b* AKG; 251 ET Archive; 252 *tl* ET Archive, *ml* AKG; 253 *t* AKG, *m* AKG, *b* ET Archive; 255 *t* ET Archive, *b* Ancient Art & Architecture Collection Ltd; 256 *tl* ET Archive, *b* Bridgeman Art Library; 257 *t* ET Archive, *b* ET Archive; 259 Bridgeman Art Library; 261 Bridgeman Art Library; 262 Bridgeman Art Library; 263 *t* Bridgeman Art Library, *m* Werner Forman Archive; 264 AKG; 266 *t* ET Archive, *b* ET Archive; 267 *t* ET Archive, *b* ET Archive; 269 Bridgeman Art Library; 272 Bridgeman Art Library; 273 *t* AKG, *m* ET Archive; 274 *t* Bridgeman Art Library, *b* Bridgeman Art Library; 275 Bridgeman Art Library; 276 ET Archive; 277 ET Archive; 278 *tl* ET Archive, *ml* Bridgeman Art Library; 282 ET Archive; 283 *t* ET Archive, *b* Bridgeman Art Library; 285 Robert Harding Picture Library; 286 Bridgeman Art Library; 288 ET Archive; 292 ET Archive; 293 ET Archive; 294 *l* Bridgeman Art Library, *b* Bridgeman Art Library; 295 *t* ET Archive, *m* ET Archive; 297 ET Archive; 298 *tl* Bridgeman Art Library, *b* Ancient Art & Architecture Collection Ltd; 300 ET Archive; 301 ET Archive; 303 ET Archive; 305 *t* Bridgeman Art Library, *b* Bridgeman Art Library; 306 ET Archive; 307 *t* ET Archive, *b* ET Archive; 309 *t* ET Archive, *b* ET Archive; 310 *tl* ET Archive, *tr* ET Archive; 311 ET Archive; 312 *tl* ET Archive, *ml* ET Archive; 313 ET Archive; 314 *ml* ET Archive, *b* ET Archive; 315 ET Archive; 323 Peter Newark's American Pictures; 324 ET Archive; 325 ET Archive; 327 *t* ET Archive, *b* ET Archive; 329 Peter Newark's American Pictures; 330 ET Archive; 331 *t* Bridgeman Art Library, *r* ET Archive, *b* ET Archive; 332 Edifile/Lewis; 336 ET Archive; 339 ET Archive; 342 Peter Newark's American Pictures; 344 *tl* ET Archive, *b* ET Archive; 345 *t* ET Archive, *b* ET Archive; 346 ET Archive; 347 *t* ET Archive, *b* ET Archive; 348 *tr* ET Archive, *b* ET Archive; 349 *t* ET Archive, *mr* ET Archive, *b* ET Archive; 351 *t* ET Archive, *m* ET Archive, *b* ET Archive; 352 ET Archive; 353 *t* ET Archive, *b* ET Archive; 355 Hulton Getty Picture Library; 356 Hulton Getty Picture Library; 357 AKG; 358 ET Archive; 359 ET Archive; 360 ET Archive; 361 ET Archive; 363 ET Archive; 364 *tr* Hulton Getty Picture Library, *ml* Hulton Getty Picture Library, *b* ET Archive; 365 ET Archive; 366 *t* Hulton Getty Picture Library, *b* ET Archive; 367 ET Archive; 368 ET Archive; 369 ET Archive; 370 *ml* Peter Newark's American Pictures, *bl* Peter Newark's American Pictures; 371 Mary Evans Picture Library; 372 ET Archive; 373 *t* Hulton Getty Picture Library, *b* ET Archive; 374 ET Archive; 375 ET Archive; 377 *t* ET Archive, *b* ET Archive; 378 *tr* ET Archive, *mr* Mary Evans Picture Library, *br* ET Archive; 379 *tl* ET Archive, *tr* ET Archive, *bl* ET Archive; 384 ET Archive; 386 ET Archive; 387 Imperial War Museum; 388 ILN; 389 *t* Hulton Deutsch Collection, *b* Hulton Getty Picture Library; 390 ET Archive; 391 *b* ET Archive; 392 Hulton Getty Picture Library; 393 Hulton Getty Picture Library; 394 *tl* ILN, *ml* ILN, *tr* ILN; 395 *tl* ET Archive, *tr* ILN, *mr* ILN; 396 *tl* Imperial War Musem, *tr* ET Archive, *b* ET Archive; 397 *tr* ET Archive, *mr* ILN; 398 *tl* ILN, *b* Hulton Deutsch Collection; 399 *t* Hulton Getty Picture Library, *mr* ET Archive, *br* ILN, *bl* ET Archive; 400 *tr* ET Archive, *ml* Corbis-Bettmann/UPI, *bl* Corbis; 401 *tr* Corbis-Bettmann, *m* Corbis, *mr* ET Archive, *bl* Corbis-Bettmann; 402 ET Archive; 403 *tr* Hulton Getty Picture Library, *br* ILN; 404 *tl* Hulton Getty Picture Library, *tr* Hulton Getty Picture Library, *bl* Hulton Getty Picture Library; 405 *mr* Corbis, *b* Novosti; 406 *tl* AKG, *ml* ILN, *b* ET Archive; 407 *t* ILN, *tr* AKG, *br* AKG; 408 *tl* ILN, *ml* ET Archive, *tr* Magnum Photos, *b* Magnum Photos; 409 *tr* ET Archive, *b* ET Archive; 410 *tl* Hulton Getty Picture Library, *b* Hulton Getty Picture Library; 411 *tr* ET Archive, *bl* Hulton Deutsch, *mb* ILN; 412 *tl* AKG, *ml* AKG, *tr* ET Archive, *b* AKG; 413 *tl* ILN, *tr* ET Archive, *b* ET Archive; 414 *tr* ILN, *b* ET Archive; 415 *tr* Imperial War Museum, *m* ILN; 416 ET Archive; 417 *tr* Imperial War Museum, *b* ET Archive; 418 *tl* ET Archive, *b* ET Archive; 419 *tl* ET Archive, *tr* ET Archive, *ml* ILN, *br* Hulton Getty Picture Library; 420 Imperial War Museum; 421 *mr* ILN, *b* Magnum Photos; 422 Hulton Deutsch Collection; 423 *tr* Hulton Getty Picture Library, *bl* Hulton Getty Picture Library; 424 *tl* Imperial War Museum, *b* Hulton Getty Picture Library; 425 ET Archive; 426 *tr* Kobal Collection, *b* AKG; 427 *tl* ILN, *tr* Corbis-Bettmann, *bl* Kobal Collection, *br* ILN; 428 *tl* ET Archive, *bl* James Neal/Arcaid, *tr* AKG, *br* Michael Jenner/Robert Harding Picture Library; 429 *tl* Richard Bryant/Arcaid, *tr* Simon Harris/Robert Harding Picture Library, *b* Steve Myerson/Robert Harding Picture Library; 430, *tr* Science Museum/Science & Society Picture Library, *bl* Science Museum/Science & Society Picture Library, *b* Quadrant Picture Library, *br* ET Archive; 431 *tl* ET Archive, *tr* ET Archive, *mr* Advertising Archives, *bl* ILN; 432 Science & Society Picture Library; 434 NASA/Science Photo Library; 435 *tl* Rex Features, *tr* Rob Francis/Robert Harding Picture Library, *br* Stuart Franklin/Magnum Photos, *bl* G.Mendel/Magnum Photos; 436 *tr* Popperfoto, *bl* Rex Features; 437 *t* Hulton Getty Picture Library, *m* Magnum Photos, *br* ET Archive, *bl* Hulton Getty Picture Library; 438 *tl* Novosti/Science Photo Library, *b* NASA/Science Photo Library; 439 *tl* NASA/Science Photo Library, *b* NASA/Science Photo Library; 440 *tl* Robert Harding, *b* Marc Riboud/Magnum Photos, *tr* Eve Arnold/Magnum Photos; 441 *tl* Stuart Franklin/Magnum Photos, *t* Stuart Franklin/Magnum Photos, *b* Paul Lowe/Magnum Photos; 442 *tr* OECD, *b* Elliot Erwitt/Magnum Photos; 443 *t* Abbas/Magnum Photos, *mr* Popperfoto/Reuters, *b* European Parliament/Airdiasol; 444 *tl* Hulton Getty Picture Library, *tr* Roger-Viollet, *bl* Corbis; 445 *t* Magnum Photos, *b* Griffiths/Magnum Photos; 446 *tl* P. Jones Griffiths/Magnum Photos, *tr* S. Franklin/Magnum Photos, *ml* Danny Lyon/Magnum, *b* Bob Adelman/Magnum Photos; 447 *t* Chris Steele-Perkins/Magnum Photos, *m* Magnum Photos, *b* Thomas Hoepker/Magnum Photos; 448 *tl* James Natchwey/Magnum Photos, *tr* Rex Features, *b* Rex Features; 449 *tr* F. Scianna/Magnum Photos, *bl* Liba Taylor/Robert Harding Picture Library, *br* Robert Harding Picture Library; 450 *tl* Hulton Getty Picture Library, *tr* Popperfoto, *b* Marilyn Silverstone/Magnum Photos; 451 *t* Pinkhassov/Magnum Photos, *m* Pinkhassov/Magnum Photos, *b* S.Franklin/Magnum Photos; 452 *tl* Burt Glinn/Magnum Photos, *b* Jones-Griffiths/Magnum Photos; 453 *t* Jean Gaumy/Magnum Photos, *mr* Stuart Franklin/Magnum, *br* Steve McCurry/Magnum Photos; 454 *tl* Hank Morgan/University of Massachusetts at Amherst/Science Photo Library, *ml* Alfred Pasieka/Science Photo Library, *b* Brian Brake/Science Photo Library, *t* Tim Davis/Science Photo Library, *tr* Dr Jeremy Burgess/Science Photo Library; 455 *t* NASA/Science Photo Library, *mr* NASA/Science Photo Library; 456 *tr* Steve McCurry/Magnum Photos, *b* Bruno Barbey/Magnum Photos; 457 *tl* G.Peress/Magnum Photos, *tr* Thomas Hopker/Magnum Photos, *bl* Russell D. Curtis/Science Photo Library, *br* Martin Bond/Science Photo Library; 458 *tl* Robert Harding Picture Library, *bl* Rob Francis/Robert Harding Picture Library, *tr* Rene Burri/Magnum Photos; 459 *ml* Micha Bar-Am/Magnum Photos, *br* Paul Lowe/Magnum Photos; 460 *tl* Steve McCurry/Magnum Photos, *tr* Paul Lowe/Magnum Photos, *b* Marilyn Silverstone/Magnum Photos; 461 *tr* Luc Delahaye/Magnum Photos, *m* Steve McCurry/Magnum Photos, *mr* Martin Parr/Magnum Photos, *b* Bruno Barbey/Magnum Photos; 462 *tl* G.Mendel/Magnum Photos, *ml* G.Mendel/Magnum Photos, *b* Frank Spooner Pictures/Gamma, *tr* Gideon Mendel/Magnum Photos; 463 Frank Spooner Pictures/Gamma, *m* Frank Spooner Pictures/Gamma, *b* Frank Spooner Pictures/Gamma; 464 *tl* Eli Reed/Magnum Photos, *b* Detlev Van Ravenwaay/Science Photo Library

Artwork archivists Wendy Allison, Steve Robinson

Editorial and design Aimee Johnson, Sheila Clewley, Julie Ferris, Emma Wilde, Dileri Johnston, Giles Sparrow, Joanne Brown

Artists Jonathan Adams, Hemesh Alles, Marion Appleton, Sue Barclay, R. Barnett, Noel Bateman, Simon Bishop, Richard Bonson, Nick Cannan, Vanessa Card, Tony Chance, Harry Clow, Stephen Conlin, Peter Dennis, Dave Etchell, Jeff Farrow, James Field, Ian Fish, Michael Fisher, Eugene Fleury, Chris Forsey, Dewey Franklin, Terry Gabbey, Fred Gambino, John Gillatt, Matthew Gore, Jeremy Gower, Neil Gower, Ray Grinaway, Allan Hardcastle, Nick Harris, Nicholas Hewetson, Bruce Hogarth, Christian Hook, Richard Hook, Simon Huson, John James, Peter Jarvis, John Kelly, Deborah Kindred, Adrian Lascombe, Chris Lenthall, Jason Lewis, Chris Lyon, Kevin Maddison, Shirley Mallinson, Shane Marsh, David MacAllister, Angus McBride, Stefan Morris, Jackie Moore, Teresa Morris, Frank Nichols, Chris D. Orr, Sharon Pallent, R. Payne, R. Philips, Jayne Pickering, Melvyn Pickering, Malcolm Porter, Mike Posen, Mike Roffe, Chris Rothero, David Salarya, Mike Saunders, Rodney Shackell, Rob Shone, Mark Stacey, Paul Stangroom, Branca Surla, Smiljka Surla, Stephen Sweet, Mike Taylor, George Thompson, Martin Wilson, David Wright, Paul Wright